Contents

Note of Hope

No matter how they otherwise think, people simply cannot possibly comprehend how sad and difficult it is when your child is born with or develops (both in our situation) a life-limiting or life-threatening illness, or what that journey and ultimate unbearable loss is truly like. They think they understand and of course try to, and do feel huge sadness (especially family and those very close), but they really do not know – nor, could they – nor would we wish or expect them to. They are just so lucky if this kind of sadness and loss hasn't darkened their doors. When a husband dies, his wife becomes a widow, and when a wife dies, her husband a widower. There is no name for parents who have lost their children, other than 'bereaved parents'.

In writing this book, my wish is that it will not be remembered as a sad book, for it is not meant to be that. There is of course, the huge sadness and loss for Brendan and me, but my hope is that overall it will be a positive and uplifting read. Most of all, that it will be a comfort and support of some kind to Mams and Dads living with very sick children who will most likely live short and difficult lives, and to those of you, who like us, have lost our precious angels. I wish most of all for a message of *hope* and *comfort* to shine through.

'When life gives 100 reasons to cry, show life 1,000 reasons to smile'

Heartfelt Thanks

I want to extend my huge and heartfelt thanks to all who have supported me through these many years. Far too numerous to mention individually, and if I mention even one, I would have to mention all, and that in itself would create a separate book. Even then, I hold a real fear that I would leave someone out and offend.

I think and hope you all know who you are and what you've done, from family and friends to people far and wide we don't even know. What you all mean to Brendan and me is beyond words, and please know this comes straight from our hearts. We have made some very special and wonderful friends, whom we will treasure for the rest of our lives. Apart from the phenomenal support to LauraLynn, we thank family and friends in particular for being there for us on a personal level, and lending us comfort, support and such caring kindness in living with our loss.

I also want to thank all who so kindly took the time to write such beautiful contributions for my book. There are many others who may have liked to contribute too, but it was impossible for me to ask everyone. Please know though, that you are all part of the book, as you are all part of our lives.

We especially thank absolutely everyone who has ever done even one small thing to make LauraLynn House become a reality, and who now help us continue to bring special care and comfort to precious little ones and their families.

'A million star-filled THANKS to one and all'

Foreword

First words are always important. This was the pressing sentiment I had when walking down Church Avenue in Blanchardstown Village – on my way to visit Jane and Brendan the day Laura died. My mind was full of pictures of innocence and bundles of joy but this! No possible joy and certainly a shattering of innocence. 'What is it I see', I thought to myself, 'when I behold a child'? The child always appeals, trusts, lacks a suspicious nature and has an ability to see the world as a place full of friends, bereft of enemies. 'How will I look them in the eye, what will I say?' I thought! Little did I know that this awful event, this early leaving was but a beginning to the deepest possible heartache, an unfolding and enveloping heartache not only for Brendan and Jane but for the wider family, for circles of friends, for the local community and well beyond. 'And Lynn', I thought, 'what about Lynn?' How could I look her in the eye and have words that might answer her questions – 'please God, she will have no questions!' She did.

Working with teenagers had given me something of an understanding around how they see the world and what is important to them. Independence, fairness and integrity, the importance of friendship and the place of generosity. Lynn, as it turned out was no different to her peers. These things were important to her too! These were her realities and her questions arose from them. How is this fair? Why did this happen? What does it mean? What about Mam and Dad? Where is Laura?

Little did she or I or anyone else know how little time there would be to begin to face these questions – for soon Lynn was facing them directly herself and for herself – how is this right, why is this happening to me, what does it mean?

It would be easy for any person to fall into an abyss of self-pity or agonizing anger or even guilt. I've oftentimes gone there myself, as no doubt some of you gentle readers have too, when life led to places we would rather not go. I suppose its part of our condition. This path, however, was not chosen by Lynn, and in saying this by the way, I'm not making her into some plaster cast saint or talking doll. I hope rather to attest to the beauty of her budding self. To be true to the trusting, hopeful, intelligent and fun young woman she was and might have further been.

Oftentimes in the course of my own calling I encounter people who never seem to grasp life, or who have difficulty in doing so. Saying this is no moral judgement, neither does it come from a superior attitude, but rather it's a statement of their reality and how the cards have fallen for them.

Lynn chose for herself another route. She grasped what she could with all her strength and might. She embraced her life and lived each moment she had. With huge foresight and deep parental love, Brendan and Jane put aside themselves and with patience, good humour and forbearance enabled

Lynn's dream and wish for herself be somewhat fulfilled. It's true to say too, that many, many others, some of whom were in the midst of their own upheavals, gave willingly and lovingly along the way. Trips and treats, concerts and celebrities, make-up and fashion provided the topics of conversation and that's exactly as it should be. A home of laughter and fun, filled with youth and vibrancy.

Sometimes, in the midst of the hurly-burly, Lynn and I had quiet moments together. In these times I had a chance to hear the talk behind the talk, the music behind the words as the cliché would say. These moments and my memory of them led me to say to an interviewer after her death, 'that there were times I felt there was a little philosopher sitting on the bed'. The depth of her engagement with her illness and the knowing of what the end would be for her both comforted and unsettled me. In saying this, though, I want to be and need to be true in remembering these precious moments. I need to be true to Lynn too. So no great revelations here save to say expressions of her deep love for Brendan and Jane, thanks for everything being done for her, regret that time was short and fear – fear not of dying for then she could 'take care of Laura', but fear of saying good-bye. How true for all of us – not wanting to say good-bye. The pain of parting! The wisdom. The humanity.

I know that Jane and Brendan, the contributors to this timely book and many others have a myriad of memories and remembrances both unsettling and comforting. Something in me is glad of course that this work has come to fruition, and I hope that it will stand as more than a mere memorial of beautiful lives cut short or wonderful parents living with the sharp paradox of the presence of an un-utterable absence, but rather a testament to bravery and young wisdom, to deep and real love and to that inspiration that we can be each to the other in our simple and respectful humanity. Believer and unbeliever alike (for want of a better phrase) can always stand together in solidarity in the face of those two mysteries that book-end our lives – namely life and death! Long may we stand together.

The request to write this foreword came unexpectedly. It has filled me with dread and I put off its writing for a long time. I'm honoured to have been asked and trust that its writing offends none. There are so many more involved in this epic story who are far more equipped than I to have dared to put pen to paper. Honoured indeed I am with this invitation, but more so honoured by the bravery of Brendan and Jane in allowing me to get to know a wonderful daughter. I mean no disregard to Laura in reserving the last comment for Lynn. 'Would you believe Lynn, I wore make-up for a whole day on the campus of Trinity College for you during the filming of *Would You Believe!*'

Kieran Dunne
Hospital Chaplain
Dublin
Summer 2015

Prologue

This is the story of the beautiful lives of my two daughters, Laura and Lynn, which were sadly all too short. Like a lot of sick children, they had courage beyond their tender years. Laura, perhaps not consciously, though I always felt she somehow did know, even at her very young age. Lynn, without doubt, in a very, very special way, as she was brave and accepting of her fate beyond belief, at the tender age of 15.

My children are my heroes, and the wind beneath my wings! They have given me the courage to carry on with a life which has lost its real meaning and, though this may sound contradictory, is still so precious. A life robbed of our darling girls and what might have been. They have given me the courage to do things I never would have attempted in my life. My girls have left a legacy, one which will outlive my husband Brendan and myself, and one with which I am very happy and proud to be associated.

Perhaps not everyone will agree – though I think most would – that our children are ultimately what our lives are all about. They are the greatest and most precious gift of all. Some people don't have children by choice, or by circumstances of life. More often than not though, the choice is taken away from them for various reasons, and I feel so sad for all in this position. Though now, and for the rest of my life, I live each day with the unbearable sadness of such loss and pain of missing my girls, I am so lucky to have the enormous joy of having had them, and the magical years with them. This by far outweighs the sadness of that enormous loss. The wonderful years we were so lucky to have had, and the even more beautiful and everlasting memories we have of them, can never be erased or taken away. We are eternally grateful for all of this, and the health we are so lucky to have in our twilight years.

This book is full of so many mixed emotions, though, like LauraLynn House, it is most of all a happy and positive story, despite the overriding sadness. First, there was joy, fun, normal family life and all that it brings. Then of course came the illnesses of Laura and Lynn, their suffering, our pain, loss, heartache and unbearable sadness, and yet smiles and fun within that mix. Lastly, there is survival, and yes fun and, strangely, a certain happiness within that too, knowing what has come from that loss – to help others in turn, and most of all, to create a legacy for our two brave, beautiful and courageous girls.

I hope you the reader will enjoy what follows, and even smile through the tears, should they fall. If you have suffered such loss, or any loss, may this book bring you comfort, courage, peace and, most of all, *hope.*

1

Jane's Story

*'Life is a cycle, always in motion. If good times have
moved on, so will times of trouble.'*
– Indian proverb

I believe that from the moment we are born, our lives are
laid out for us, which doesn't make it any easier for me to
understand my path to date. Life surely is a 'mystery'! We
do have choices of course, but for the most part I think fate
dictates the choices we make. The 'Sliding Door' syndrome –
if we'd gone this way or that – what if?

Our path is a hard one without doubt, and not one I would
wish for anyone, but having said that, I know there are many
people in this world far worse off than us, and people who
have had, or may be experiencing, very difficult and often
horrific lives. This world is often a hugely complicated, sad
and difficult place. However, it is also a place of great beauty,
amazing happenings and experiences, and truly wonderful
people. For the most part, I love life and the people in my life,
despite the heartache I live with. I guess, regardless of its ups

and downs, this is the only life we have, and we only get one shot at it. We should try to make the best of it, especially if we are lucky enough to have our health, something no money can buy, and no medics can fix either, on occasion.

I never thought anyone would be interested in my personal story, but I have been advised otherwise by those who know, so I hereby comply and include some background information.

I was born on 2 March 1954 into a middle class family. Mam was from Meath, and Dad from Tralee, County Kerry. He had come to Dublin to work in the Civil Service aged 18. There are four of us in the family. I have one older brother and two younger.

We were lucky to have had parents who made sure we received a good education, and all went on to do well in life, found good secure jobs, when that may have been easier than it is now. We had our ups and downs, and I wouldn't say my childhood or early teenage years were idyllic, but every family has its problems.

I was a good student, and studied hard. I loved school, though I did leave after my Intermediate (now Junior) Certificate, went on to Commercial College, and then on to work. My first job (apart from a part time job at Woolworths, while still at school) was as a Laboratory Assistant in the Bon Secours Hospital, Glasnevin. Then I followed the family tradition and joined the Civil Service. My Dad, uncles and two brothers were Civil Servants, so I guess it was not surprising. I worked in the Department of Environment (then Local Government), for the first three years in O'Connell Bridge House, followed by eight happy years in the Minister's Office, Custom House.

I enjoyed my work and colleagues very much. The work was interesting and varied, especially working in the Minister's Office – it was a great eight years. I got on with colleagues, and had one or two special friends along the way. It was there I was to meet my closest friend Dolores, and little did we know just how much we would share through the years, especially the loss of our eldest daughters to the same condition. Just as well we can't see into the future!

We had some fun times together, though Dolores married young and had her two daughters Lorraine and Gillian pretty quickly, and had left work after the second one. We saw a lot of each other through the years though, and were always very close, and I loved her gorgeous daughters. We had a great friendship, and share many stories and life experiences.

My Mam died from lung cancer when I was 20 and she just 50. It was a difficult time for us all, and we missed her dearly. It was sometime later, especially when I married and had my girls, that I truly missed her. We were close, but I reckon would have been far closer in the coming years, and she would have been there for me when I had my angels.

I think on reflection that we should all have had the option of bereavement counselling. It was never mentioned and probably wasn't available in the way it is in recent years. Illness, particularly cancer, death and loss were kind of taboo subjects, and the thinking seemed to be, sad yes, but let's not talk about it. Now, get up and just get on with life. As anyone who has been bereaved in any way knows (which is pretty much most families), it is easier said than done to just get on with it. I firmly believe in counselling, speaking about your loss, and always remembering that special person or people in our lives. Particularly our parents – part of our lives for so long –should never be forgotten, even if only now with us in spirit. Crying for that lost person, but smiling too at past lovely memories, is also so healthy.

I met Brendan when I was about 19, having had a few boyfriends in the previous years. I guess I really liked him straight away, and had known him to see, as we lived close to each other. The reason we met was a sad one really, as Brendan's Mam had come to our house to see my Mam, who had lung cancer, and that was how the connection was made. I joked many years later that I would cite Molly in our divorce proceedings, as she had secretly planned the whole thing originally. Our relationship was great, we really got on so well and grew to love each other (though I suppose it included lust in those days too, as it does with most young couples). We had a few ups, downs and break away times, but eventually got married, seven years after meeting.

Our early years, before we had children, were mixed with all sorts of emotions with getting used to being married and learning to live together, when we'd both come straight from our family homes. I suppose I was a little more prepared, as I had been the 'Mam' in my house, since my Mam had died. The housework, cooking, etc. was something I had long been doing, so none of it was alien to me. Anyway, I eventually got pregnant with darling Lynn, had her, loved her so, and we watched her grow with great pride and immense joy. How quickly the years pass!

When Lynn was four, we moved house because the school Lynn was going to attend was in Glasnevin. Lynn loved school, made friends easily and was a good student and popular young girl. She always longed for a little sister and would often voice this to me. We didn't plan or not plan to have another baby, but it happened when I was 40, and I always remember friends saying to me, be careful, now you're into your forties, and I had just laughed. But they were right, and so many couples 'get caught', as I've since discovered. I was delighted though, even if a little concerned, because of my age.

Lynn was thrilled and her close friend Siobhán was longing for her Mam to have another baby too, as she only had an older brother. The pregnancy went fine and all seemed well, and Laura was born on 20 January 1995, a Friday evening, at approximately 8.30 pm. I gave anyone who wanted one a celebratory drink, plenty of time on this occasion. The birth was so easy compared to Lynn – no haemorrhaging and not so many stitches – a breeze! However, sadly, on the following day Laura was diagnosed with Tetralogy of Fallot, a congenital heart condition. We were shocked, upset and it was a difficult time for us all. However, Laura did not have to stay in Our Lady's Hospital, where she had now become a patient, but we could bring her home – a big plus, as not everyone gets so lucky.

Life went on, and we had our ups and downs, with Laura spending six months at, and two surgeries in, Our Lady's Hospital in the first year of her little life – sometimes we thought she would not make it, but she did, thankfully. The next few years were pretty good (and relatively 'normal'), and we had a nice family life again. Then Laura's condition deteriorated and Lynn also developed a serious illness, and that was the start of the road we would not wish on anyone. The rest is history now and told in the stories that follow.

2

That Awful Night

'Storm in my heart
Tearing me apart
Storm in my heart'
– Colin Hay

We put one foot in front of the other. How we stood, never mind walk, I'll never know. We had just received the news that Lynn had leukaemia, and were walking now to St. John's Oncology Ward in Our Lady's Hospital for sick children in Crumlin.

Lynn, aged 13, had started her second year in secondary school that day - 30 August 1999. It was 5.30 pm that fateful evening when she and her Dad arrived to await the outcome of her little sister Laura's final heart surgery. Laura had gone to theatre about an hour earlier, and as Lynn was looking a little peaky, we decided to have her checked out in Casualty. She had not been complaining of feeling unwell, but didn't object to having the checkup. Having had bloods taken and various other procedures, we sat in the old hallway, which was quiet and peaceful, to await news of Laura. At this point in time, we were not at all worried about Lynn, probably thinking, if anything, she was anaemic or something minor.

We were called back to Casualty, and brought to a type of sitting room off the main area. Looking back, it is a wonder how I never for one minute even had any inclination there might be anything seriously wrong. However, as we sat down on a couch, Brendan and I, either side of Lynn, we surely must have suspected something? Here was the casualty team, our cardiac liaison nurse, and other people we didn't know. It turned out these were the Oncologist and a nurse from St. John's Ward, who were there to tell us the shocking news that Lynn had leukaemia. Lynn just let out a little cry and I just sat there, picturing my friend's daughter who was dying from leukaemia in another Dublin hospital. I clearly remember the thought pounding in my head that this just could not be happening! But very sadly, of course, it was.

Lynn asked the Consultant three questions. Would she lose her hair? Would she have her own room? The third one, which we knew later really astounded him, would she need a bone marrow transplant? As it happened, the type of leukaemia Lynn had didn't initially need a bone marrow transplant? He wondered how this 13-year-old girl knew anything about bone marrow, or hair loss, but of course, at that time, he didn't know how much we knew about leukaemia. Lynn was admitted there and then to the Oncology Ward – St John's.

As we walked that long corridor to the other end of the hospital, and into St. John's, I was thinking how far away from the rest of the hospital it seemed, and wondered sometime later if it was to do with the often emaciated look of the children, with their bald heads and almost yellow pallor of their faces. We had seen one or two, a few years earlier, when we had spent six months on the Cardiac Ward with Laura. I remember mentioning it once, and was assured it wasn't so. Strangely, though, it was the same in the hospital where my friend's daughter Lorraine received her treatment! Anyway, I guess it doesn't really matter, at the end of the day. I vaguely remember it being very quiet, probably, without meaning to sound dramatic, even a little eerie. That was possibly to do with the way we were feeling anyhow. We passed one or two people on the way, but as it was quite late, not too many people were moving around. It seemed so cold, drab – an endless path, as if we were heading to the ends of the earth, and in a way, I guess we were!

I wondered what darling Lynn was thinking. Her mind must have been a whirl of so many emotions and worries, picturing her adored friend so ill with the leukaemia now invading her own body. I was later to recall her words on her last visit to Lorraine, not so long beforehand. We were driving home after the visit, and she said, 'Mam, I was just thinking, what if I got leukaemia?' My answer, which I firmly believed, was 'How would that ever happen – of course not?' She possibly already had it there and then. She also, without doubt, was so worried about her little sister up in ICU. She was only 13 years old. She should not have to bear such awful burdens. It was all so unfair and unbearable, and though I don't recall feeling it, there must have been such a sense of despair for all three of us.

We were 'lucky' to get our own room (a double one, at that), and were to quickly learn that this was a fairly rare occurrence. It just happened to be quiet there that night, and because of our special circumstances, I believe the wonderful caring staff wanted to do as much as they could to make us 'comfortable'. We also learned way later, that a Dad and his daughter (who sadly didn't survive long term either), gave up the much coveted double room for us, and also made up the fold up beds for Brendan and me. That was such a very kind and caring thing to do, and we have never forgotten it.

We had some tea and toast, without ever tasting any of it, and tried to rest. Poor darling Lynn – she got into that bed, and how she must have been so confused, shocked and worried, not just about herself, but about Laura too. We were all thinking of how our little Shirley Temple was doing, and still had great hope at this point.

So began the long cancer road for Lynn, before we even knew how the other road would end.

3

Laura's Story

'Time is a gift. The heart is like a clock – set at a certain time to start, and a certain time to stop.'

The date was 20 January 1995 – the wonderful and exciting day of the birth of our beautiful daughter Laura. It was almost 8.30 pm on a Friday evening, and I was so happy. I couldn't wait to tell Lynn, whom I knew had longed so much for a little sister. She was almost nine then. Sadly, though, our happiness wasn't to last long. On Saturday morning, when the paediatrician examined Laura, she thought she heard a murmur on the heart, and although this can sometimes occur, she had another specialist check her out later. Following this, Laura was taken up to a special unit in the hospital for a more thorough check. I guess at this stage, the experts already knew something was wrong. As it happened, the unit was busy, and Laura was brought back to me just in time for visiting. Brendan and Lynn were first in and it was great to see Lynn's excitement on seeing her long awaited for little sister. Thankfully, I had Laura back, as I had so many visitors that afternoon. Later on, she was again taken up to the unit, and by visiting time that evening (7.00 pm) she was still there. I suppose I should have guessed then that something was wrong, but I didn't. I had just my brother and a few friends in to visit, and was anxious to show off my beautiful little angel, so I asked Brendan to see about having her returned to us. He went off to enquire, and didn't return until almost 8.00 pm. Again, I didn't realise there was anything up, although at this stage, Brendan knew there was a problem. I often wondered how it was I didn't guess. I suppose you're not really with it, or maybe just don't want to think about it! When the visitors had gone, Brendan was just about to tell me something was wrong, when the doctor from the special unit came along and explained that Laura had some sort of heart problem, although at this point he didn't know exactly what it was. The shock of this was enormous, especially as we knew nothing about heart problems in children at this point in time, but boy, did we learn about them pretty quickly.

I was brought up to the unit a while later and looked at my little baby in an incubator, although she wasn't on oxygen or needing any help breathing. I cried so much, as I didn't understand any of this nightmare. Our great joy snatched away so quickly. We were asked if we wanted to name our baby and as we hadn't really thought of it much before, we decided on Laura – no reason why, except we didn't want her going to Our Lady's Hospital without a name, and that's where she was heading later that night with Brendan and one of the nurses, to have her heart checked out on an Echo heart machine, to see exactly what the problem was.

After they left, and I had to go back to the ward alone and listen to the other babies crying, was one of the loneliest points in my life. Eventually, after a few hours (about 2.30 a.m.) Brendan came back from Our Lady's, minus our beautiful baby. The doctor came and explained to us that Laura had a condition called Tetralogy of Fallot, which is basically a hole in the heart, and narrowing of the arteries around the heart. He didn't know a whole lot about it, but we would be told by the experts in Our Lady's. Needless to say, I didn't spend a lot of time sleeping in what was left of that night, and I cried many more tears, but the following morning I tried to pull myself together, and somehow come to terms with what was happening, even though I really didn't quite understand the enormity of it at that point.

Luckily, I was well enough later on when Brendan came in to go to Our Lady's with him. I couldn't wait to see my little Laura again and hold her in my arms. She looked lovely and was in a little room on St. Teresa's Ward, not needing any kind of support. She was being fed by a lovely nurse, who I'll always remember so well. The Consultant Paediatrician, one of the nicest people I have ever met, came to see us and explained Laura's condition to us in more detail. It didn't seem so bad at that stage. She would have to have an operation in the first year of her life to insert a shunt in her heart, until the major surgery for a full repair could be carried out eventually. At that time, it looked like it would be between the ages of two and three approximately. And so, we took Laura home the following day, and got on with life, which was fairly normal for the next seven months. Laura was pretty well, except for some 'spells', which were similar to colic. She ate very well, and we were lucky in that, as most 'heart children' are not great feeders. She thrived and grew, and was cute and funny and so loveable with her mop of curly hair – a real Shirley

Temple. We all adored her, especially Lynn, who finally had the little sister she had waited for so long.

Laura's first surgery eventually came along on 27 August 1995, and of course we were very worried, but Laura was so strong we felt she would be okay. Lynn went to stay with her best friend Siobhan and her family (who are like our second family). The operation was performed by Mr. Maurice Neligan who was such a lovely man. The surgery itself went well, or so it appeared, but on the following day (Thursday) Laura was not responding in the way that would have been expected. Mr. Neligan was called back in that evening and Laura was again brought to theatre at approximately 7.30 p.m. He thought perhaps that the original shunt was blocked, but on opening Laura he found this was not the problem. He then proceeded to open and close her several times, and had almost reached the point of considering the full heart repair when he finally discovered that a clot had gone through the shunt and into an artery. Thankfully, he managed to save Laura's life, when there really seemed little hope. It took a long time in I.C.U. and a lot of ventilation before Laura began to come around, and eventually she came off the ventilator, but our problems were far from over.

We would get Laura home every so often, but we always ended up bringing her back, with an infection of one kind or another. Lynn, in the meantime, was so good in coping with everything, and was doing a fairly big musical with her drama group, 'The Broadway Story', which was on for a full week, every night. We actually had Laura home at this stage for the longest time we had ever had her, but as the week went on, she was going down a little. Eventually, on the night of 10 December, at about 3.00 a.m., we had to rush to Our

Lady's with her. This time we almost left it too late, as Laura's breathing was very bad and she had to go back to I.C.U. and on to a ventilator, the furthest she had ever deteriorated since her first surgery. At almost the same moment, Brendan was called to the office on St. Brigid's Ward to take a phone call, which was to tell him that his mother had died in Our Lady's Hospice. She had had cancer for a number of years and had been in the Hospice for the previous ten days or so, but it was the actual timing which was so strange and so very sad. Eventually we got home at about 7.00 am in the morning, and Brendan's sister Irene and her husband Frank had gone to our house and were there with Lynn.

Meanwhile, we had to arrange a funeral for Brendan's mother and were back in the hospital with Laura, once again quite ill. The decision was then made to remove the top lobe of Laura's right lung, as it was reckoned that problems after her first surgery had caused huge damage to her lung, and this operation would help her. I couldn't help thinking that it might also kill her, as she certainly hadn't got the same strength she once had. Anyway, we didn't have a lot of choice, and the operation went ahead. Brendan couldn't be there on the day, and my friend Dolores came to the hospital to be with me. Laura went to theatre in the morning, and as we said goodbye to her, I felt so frightened she wouldn't recover. We were given a beeper and told to go off for a walk or whatever and if there was a problem they would contact us. We went to a local coffee shop and waited with dread for the beeper to go off. Thankfully, it didn't and we returned to the hospital to find Laura was out of surgery and was going back to I.C.U. She looked so frail when I first saw her, and my heart was breaking for my beautiful little angel.

However, always the little fighter, she fought hard, and although she wasn't great, she managed to go on. Christmas was not a good time, and Christmas Day was very sad with Santa coming to I.C.U. to see Laura. Of course, she didn't understand him then anyway, but that particular Santa photo is so terribly poignant. I guess we were wondering too if there would ever be a 'proper' one. Anyhow, Christmas passed and New Year came, and Laura wasn't so well. On New Year's night, we were standing at her bedside in St. Pat's I.C.U. and noticed she was not breathing, even though the staff said she was. There was a sort of controlled panic and we were asked to wait in a little room down the corridor. Eventually, they seemed to get it under control, and Laura was comfortable again, but we were so upset by the whole episode as we thought she wasn't going to make it, once more.

Time went on and she improved a lot. One of the nurses, whose name escapes me right now, was determined to get her off the ventilator before her birthday and she persevered so much that she succeeded. It was wonderful to be able to hold her again properly and to know that she could breathe again on her own. By the time of Laura's first birthday on January 20, she was doing really well and had a little birthday party on the ward. By the beginning of February or so, Laura was allowed home. One part of us was so happy, and the other was wondering how long we would get at home this time. However, we were pleasantly surprised, as Laura started to pick up and although she still had a feed tube in, we were determined to get her feeding normally again. So, we got the bright idea of liquidising her food and, using a huge syringe, we managed to get food into her mouth, and got her to swallow it. She had been so used to having to be suctioned, and had had a feed tube in for so long, she had a fear of actually eating, and I suppose had forgotten how to eat. It was wonderful to have her back to 'normal' again. Lynn was so happy to have her little sister home and to have some sort of a normal house and life again. It had been so hard on her and you almost forget the other child or children when you're dealing with a seriously ill baby, who is always the priority.

Laura continued to thrive and went from strength to strength. She did find the house strange as, of course, the hospital had been the only 'home' she knew for so long. She grew well, looked prettier each day, with her mop of curly hair growing well again. She started to walk and ate well (with a little encouragement) and was funny and cute and loved by all, most especially me, her Dad and big sister, Lynn. Life went on as 'normal', although I do remember in the early days of having Laura home I was quite nervous, because she was so frail, and I was alone with her and couldn't ring a bell, should anything go wrong. Having said that, it was still so great not having to travel back and forth to Crumlin, and to be out of that hospital and in our own home again. We had basically spent the last six to seven months there.

Lynn went to school and looked forward to seeing Laura on her return each day and we enjoyed our weekends and tried to get out and about, so Laura could see a bit of the world she had missed for so long. Life was as normal and good as it could be at that stage, although Laura's breathing was still laboured and, of course, she still had a hole in her heart which would need to be repaired in the future and caused her to be somewhat limited in life. We were so used to her breathing and her looking a little blue, but family and friends would see her in a much worse light than we did. I often tell the story of how Lynn took her for a walk one day to the local shop and a lady stopped to look at her in the buggy, saying how pretty she was and then heard her laboured breathing, and asked Lynn if she had asthma. Lynn said very matter of factly, that no, she just had a hole in the heart, at which the lady looked a little shocked and taken aback, not surprisingly. We often laugh about that now. Laura would have to go for regular visits to Our Lady's and in fact on her first visit in the March of '96, she picked up an infection and ended up back in for about a week. We always hated the visits, for fear of infection and also hated to see her having to have blood taken, as she naturally feared the needles, and who could blame her, after all she had been through in her little life to date, and with her tiny little veins.

The next few years passed and life went on in a fairly normal way. Laura got infections from time to time, but thankfully we managed them quite well ourselves and for the most part she was pretty well – she grew into such a beautiful little girl, with her mass of curls, full of fun and a great zest for life. I often think now that she almost knew her little life would be short and so enjoyed every minute, without having very much of anything. Lynn went on to finish her Primary at NDNSP (Educate Together School) and she and I went to London for a few days when she was 12. It was good for her to be given treats and have some special time just for her (not that she ever complained or looked for it), as Laura had taken the limelight in every way in her short life to date, understandably so. Lynn loved the theatre and still attended her own Drama group, which she loved. We went to a couple of shows in the West End, and had such a fun time – just the two of us – very special (although I didn't know just how special then). Lynn spent a lot of time with her close friend Sibhy (Siobhán), mostly out in her house in Malahide and also on holiday with the family in Cork and Spain. Sibhy would also spend quite a bit of time with us and meanwhile they both started second level school, albeit in different schools – our girls were growing up fast.

In the summer of 1999, Laura was set to go in for the final repair to her heart on July 19 (having been cancelled on many occasions through the previous years). Lynn went to Spain with her 'other' family for that month. As it happened, we had gone in to Our Lady's and Laura was prepared for surgery, and we waited and waited, when at last, once again, we were cancelled, due to an emergency case. I remember being distraught at the time, as the preparation and overnight stay is such an ordeal, but as things turned out, we were very glad of the extra time we got. It was a lovely summer, with lots of sunshine, and we all missed Lynn so much, but enjoyed the days with Laura and got out and about at the weekends.

The next date we got for Laura's surgery was 30 August, so not too much delay this time. Lynn had come back from Spain, and almost straight off (having missed the first week), she and Sibhy went off to Cul Aodh, a Gaeltacht in West Cork, which they had attended the previous year and, of course, loved. We dropped them off and had a weekend ourselves with Laura – she was so excited, as it was the furthest she had travelled in her little life, so a great adventure for her. We took the girls out for a few hours on the Sunday, before heading back to Dublin. Back home, I got on with organising Lynn's school books and so on, as she would be starting her second year in secondary school on August 30. Lynn came back from the Gaeltacht on the weekend that Laura was going in to prepare again for her final surgery, but she chose to spend Saturday out in Malahide and would meet us at the hospital on Sunday, when I had to go in with Laura for the overnight stay.

Sunday came and we headed over to Crumlin in the early afternoon, wondering if this time the operation would go ahead on Monday. Laura was prepared for surgery the following morning, with the nightmare of the cannula being inserted – she had, as mentioned previously, developed a real fear of needles and it is very difficult to insert cannulas in such small veins, and particularly difficult in 'heart' children. Some are pretty expert and some pretty awful, so it all depends on who's inserting – not their fault, I guess, as it's not easy. With Laura too, even when it's in place, she still hated them going near it, as she assumed it was going to hurt all over again. Anyway, we got it sorted and 'settled' in, while trying to occupy Laura as the hours passed. Our friends, Phil and Con, arrived over late evening with Siobhān and Lynn, as Lynn was starting second year in Dominican College, Cabra, the following day. They brought Laura a gorgeous new nightdress, which she was so excited about and put on immediately, and she did a little dance. A doctor from the surgical team came in to have us sign papers, and was very pessimistic at Laura's chances, as the surgeon had been back in July, so this was quite disconcerting for us. Brendan and Lynn stayed a little longer and then said their 'goodbyes' to Laura. I gave Lynn a big hug and said we'd see her after school the next day. I then tried to get Laura to settle and she eventually did, and I tried to settle down on the floor in a sleeping bag of sorts, supplied by the ward, and which was, to put it mildly, a tad uncomfortable. However, I guess tiredness overcomes us all, and I must have got some sleep, I'm sure, as did Laura, thankfully.

Monday morning, August 30, dawned early, and the hospital was buzzing around 6.00 am, as hospitals are wont to do – no lying-in here, even if you could or would want to! Laura was, of course, fasting, so I had to try to keep her occupied and steer her away from wanting food, and keep my mind off the surgery to come. Little did I know this was the day that would change our lives forever.

We were fourth on the list, and when Brendan arrived in about 1.00 pm, we were still not looking good to go. We asked to speak to our Consultant, and told him our fears at the pessimism being shown from the surgical team. He assured us as best he could and we knew we had little choice, as Laura's only chance was to repair her heart defect. At about 3.00 pm, it was decided that Brendan should go collect Lynn after school.

Brendan had just left, when it was decided that the child in front of Laura was to be cancelled, so we were definitely next. I was so sorry Brendan was gone, and asked if we could call home for Laura to say goodbye to her Dad and Linnie, as she called her sister. I'll always remember her words to Lynn: 'Bye Linnie – I'm going to get fixed now.' They were the last words she ever said to Lynn, and the last time she spoke to her Daddy too.

She was excited to go for a ride on the trolley, but I could also sense a little fear in her – she probably felt my fear and sadness at having to take her into theatre, though I tried hard not to show it. It is such an awful feeling, leaving your baby in that pre-theatre, in the hands of a total stranger. Luckily, an old school friend who had nursed for many years there, and was now head of Admissions, was waiting for me outside theatre, and helped console me a little.

We went for tea, and waited for Brendan and Lynn to arrive, which they did soon after. Lynn was hungry, so we went to have some food in the canteen, though Lynn didn't actually eat very much in the end. Brendan had mentioned to me how he thought she had been looking a little pale recently, in the small amounts of time we had seen her in the previous weeks, but I had put it down to her being tired after a month of late nights in Spain and the Gaeltacht. She wasn't complaining and had quite a tan, so I didn't take too much notice of her pallor. However Brendan mentioned it to our friend, and suggested Lynn go to Casualty, and while she did agree with him, tried to put us off, as she felt we had enough on our plate with Laura in theatre. However, he persisted and she said she would organise it for us.

They took bloods and a couple of young doctors came and mentioned a rash on Lynn's body, which was there but barely visible, so we hadn't noticed. Her nose and gums were also bleeding a little, and we did see bruises on her arms then, which we hadn't seen before either. Unfortunately, my close friend Dolores' daughter Lorraine was very ill in another hospital with leukaemia, and we knew bruising was one of the signs there. We both admitted later that it crossed our minds, but we never voiced it to each other then. We went off to the quiet old hallway to sit and wait for word of Laura, and even saw the surgeon who had performed Laura's surgery going home about 9.00 pm, so felt positive enough about that. Shortly after, we were called back to Casualty to find not only the Cardiac team there, but also a team from

Oncology, who told us as gently as they could that Lynn had leukaemia. I will never forget those words, as all I could think of was Lorraine, so ill in James's hospital (she was to die 10 weeks later, on her 22nd birthday). We didn't know what was happening in theatre with Laura, and now we had to deal with this horrific news – I'll never know to this day how any of us coped, especially darling Lynn, who adored Lorraine, and now had to face the same illness, with her baby sister upstairs in theatre, and none of us knowing how she was doing. Lynn was admitted to St. John's Ward there and then, and we had no idea what was happening to Laura, now in I.C.U.

People often ask, 'how did you feel – what went through your mind'? Well, that's a very hard question to answer, as I think we were all in such shock. I remember looking at a picture on the wall in that sitting room, and thinking of how ill Lorraine was (she being the only person we knew with leukaemia at this point), and now Lynn had the same disease. Lynn just cried briefly, before asking the Consultant those three questions – would she lose her hair, would she have her own room, and would she need a bone marrow transplant? Then, we just got up, put one foot in front of the other, and walked the long corridor to the other end of the hospital, and into St. John's Ward – Oncology.

It was about 11.30 pm when Brendan and I were asked to come up to I.C.U to see Laura and talk to the member of the Cardiac team, the one who had been so very negative, the day before. He wasn't any more positive this time, and told us that the surgeon had managed to do the full repair, but that Laura was very ill. We expected that any little body that had gone through such serious surgery would be just that, so still had our own hope that she would come through.

However, when we went into the I.C.U there was something different about her that we hadn't seen after her previous two surgeries – she looked pretty lifeless and was so very cold. Our poor tiny little doll – my heart broke and my arms ached to hold her. We whispered to her to be strong and then had to go back to Lynn, as we didn't want her to be alone. It was all such a terrible nightmare, and you wished you could just wake up and everything would be fine – such heartache, and such a feeling of loss, as to what to do next, torn between the two. We got back to Lynn and all tried to 'sleep', but I'm guessing none of us really did.

At about 5.30 am, Brendan and I were called back to I.C.U. to be told the dreaded news that Laura was not responding well and instead of weaning her off some drugs, they were having to give her more, and her kidneys were failing. We knew it wasn't very hopeful, though we had to try to keep some of the hope alive for Laura. We went back down to St. John's, and tried to 'sleep' some more. I don't remember, but I think we got some tea and toast at some point.

At about 9.00 am, we were again called up to I.C.U. to be told the horrific news that our baby was brain dead, and that we needed to think about taking her off life support. At that point in my life, it was the worst moment. We felt so hopeless and so helpless. A little later we had to make the decision whether to allow the oncologist to see if he might take enough bone marrow from Laura, in the event that she might be a match for Lynn who might relapse after her first round of treatment. Again, we were to learn much later that there was a huge chance Lynn would relapse, as can happen quite often, sadly. But I guess we had enough on our plates at that time, and really didn't need or want to know what else could or might happen in the future.

This might seem like an easy decision, given that Laura was not going to open her eyes again. She never did, and I always felt she died on the day of surgery – the machines really kept her alive. However, we felt (irrationally, I guess) this might cause Laura more 'hurt' or pain, as they were to turn her over on her front, and stick large needles in her little back. We were assured though that this was not so, and I remember saying to Brendan that if Laura could make this decision she would want to give Lynn every chance, and if her bone marrow helped, then please take it.

As it happened, the Consultant did a needle biopsy, and knew he would not get enough, so there was no point in trying, so that was one decision taken from our hands. We had to tell Lynn that Laura would not wake up and I can't remember how sad she looked or what she said – I think she cried a little, but I do know how her little heart must surely have been breaking, and how she was now so ill herself. What an enormous shock and horror for a 13-year-old girl to have to deal with.

We decided to hold a little Confirmation ceremony for Laura later that morning in the I.C.U., and Lynn and her friend Sibhy, whose family had come to the hospital (along with other family and friends), came into I.C.U. with us. It was so very sad, and Lynn gave Laura her own name in Confirmation and was her Sponsor. It was also very comforting, in a strange sort of way.

At this point, we still had to make the decision of when to take Laura off ventilation and let her die naturally. Oh! What a huge sorrow! We made the decision early afternoon, and I remember asking Lynn to come back up with us, as I thought she would always regret it if she wasn't with her little beloved Laura at the very end. She got a little upset though, and said she had seen her and said her 'goodbyes', so would leave it. I told her we would wait a while in I.C.U., and if she changed her mind, to come on up. She did just that, as I kind of thought she might, and I am so glad to this day that she did.

We were told that Laura would take a while to die, but as I took her in my arms, when all those tubes had been removed, she was already 'asleep' for evermore. She looked just like a little doll – beautiful and serene – our little Shirley Temple – gone now to her new home. I wished I could keep her little body with me always – such a silly thought really, but it didn't seem that way then. We stayed a while and then Laura was laid in a little room off I.C.U., where we could come and visit her anytime at all. She looked like a little doll, sound asleep for now, not dead asleep forever.

We went back to Oncology to get on with Lynn's already started treatment and I can't remember much more of that day. I know friends and family came and went, and I don't know how many times we went up to I.C.U. to see Laura, with other people and alone, but I think it was quite a lot. I guess we spoke about what we would do, and Lynn didn't want Laura to go home, so we decided to have her laid out in the little chapel room at Our Lady's the following day and bring her to our church in Blanchardstown the next evening.

If it was now, I know we would have had just one service, with burial afterwards, but I guess we weren't thinking straight at all, and back then it was the way it was. I think Brendan and I came back home that evening, leaving poor

Lynn alone in that hospital with Laura resting upstairs. I suppose we had to do practical things, albeit in slow motion and working mechanically. It was so strange to be in our own home again, as the last time we had been there our lives were so different – all this horror, in only a few days.

The saying, 'We never know what tomorrow will bring' is so terribly true. I use the word 'terrible', as sadly, that's often what tomorrow brings – something awful. We again went through the motions of showering, shaving (in Brendan's case) and changing our clothes, then gathering up some things for us and for Lynn, and headed back to the hospital. At this point, the car could probably have gone alone, it had already done the journey what seemed like a million times, especially in the first six to seven months of Laura's original time there.

I really can't remember how Lynn was, other than to know how sad and awful it had to be for her, especially. I remember she didn't really talk too much about Laura, and one of her nurses told me she had come in to the room, once or twice, and knew Lynn had been crying, but would try to cover up in front of her. In recent years, however, I was to meet one of the nurses from Oncology again, who had looked after Lynn. She told me that Lynn had spoken to her and one or two others about Laura, and this has meant so much to me. At least she managed to share her sadness and loss with someone.

I felt so heartbroken for my beautiful daughter at that time, and always so sad that I could not take away her pain. They had started treatment from that first night and she was pretty weak and sore, poor angel. As far as I can recall, I stayed that night, as I think we still had the room to ourselves, which was a minor miracle for which we were very grateful.

We tried to sleep, and probably did somewhat, only through pure physical and mental exhaustion. I'm sure I cried and cried, as I did a lot in those days and for many more days, months and years ahead, but again, I can't consciously recall precisely.

Next morning, we got up and used the hospital facilities, which at that time left a lot to be desired. I remember being in the shower, crying again, and feeling that I must be in a very bad nightmare – this just didn't seem real, and yet I knew it was. It was a feeling of total unreality, once again, impossible to explain.

Brendan came over to the hospital and we decided to hold a little service for Laura that afternoon, and had to go home to get the clothes we were to dress her in. I can't clearly remember the sequence of events, but I recall dressing our little angel in a beautiful dress she had worn on Lynn's Confirmation day. I brushed her beautiful curls and she still looked like a doll – Brendan took some photos, which I have only looked at once or twice – too difficult to do so, but still special to have. We laid her in her little coffin in the small chapel room, and it was heartbreaking saying a last 'goodbye' and kissing our beautiful angel. Our hearts were literally broken in two. We returned to St. John's Ward then.

The service was held about 4.00 pm and family, friends and quite a lot of staff came to be with us and pay their respects. Many tears were shed, and my heart was even more broken for Lynn, who was so sad, shocked and so ill too. After others had left the chapel, Brendan, Lynn and I, with a few close family, said our final goodbyes and gave our final kisses to Laura. Closing the lid of her little white coffin was at that point one of the most awful moments, one of the hardest things we ever had to do. We made the journey, with our little angel's coffin in our car, to our church in Blanchardstown Village, and we were lucky to have a wonderful priest Kieran, a friend who we knew and liked greatly (See Foreword.)

I don't remember this at all, but apparently, we carried the little coffin ourselves to the altar. The service was lovely and afterwards Kieran explained that Brendan, Lynn and I apologised, but had to return straight back to Our Lady's, and we went out the back of the altar and never looked back. I hated leaving Laura alone, although I suppose it was nice she was in the peaceful surroundings of the church.

Poor Lynn was quite weak and so very tired, and we slept somewhat that night. We left early next morning to go home and get ready for the funeral we were dreading. We got to the church and somehow got through the Mass, which was very sad and difficult. Even more difficult was the burial – Laura was buried with my parents in Glasnevin cemetery. Again, because Lynn was very weak and had to return to Our Lady's, it is a funeral we barely remember. Laura was laid down and prayers said, and we literally got back in the car and drove straight back to the hospital. I don't remember much of the rest of that day or how we felt, but I know it was so very, very sad.

Our little angel had gone to Heaven and it was now time to get on with Lynn's treatment and help her get better. We didn't have time to grieve for Laura then. I remember walking the long corridor to St. John's Ward in the following days, and thinking, 'will I ever see the end of this place?' When we were on the Cardiac Ward with Laura, we would occasionally see a bald-headed child, and I always remember feeling so sad for them – little did I know then what was ahead.

I remember the days shortly after Laura died, and I would go to the local shop around the corner from Our Lady's to get something for Lynn. The locals would be taking their children to school, and I would think it all so surreal, and wonder how could they not know what was going on in my life? How I'd already lost one little angel and my other was now so sick. I would hear one shout (reasonably so really) at their child, or see a child upset, and feel so angry, I would almost scream out loud. How could they be acting so normally? I know it was so silly and irrational of me, as of course they couldn't have known, but I almost hated them for that.

4

Lynn's Story

*'Some things are more precious because
they don't last'* – Oscar Wilde

We were six years married when we had Lynn, and I remember feeling so, so happy I had my little girl, as I secretly wanted a girl, so much. The date – 11 March 1986. It was a tough birth and I haemorrhaged quite badly afterwards. I really thought I was going to die, though the anaesthetist assured me otherwise, and thankfully he was right. However, I did haemorrhage again two weeks later, and returned to the Rotunda Hospital for a few more days, due to having a D&C.

The first three to four months were pretty tough, as I think they are for most new parents, especially Mams, who've also got the physical scars to deal with, particularly first time round. However, time does heal certain things, and as time went on, and once Lynn began to sleep through the night, life started to get back to normal. We began to really enjoy our beautiful little girl. She was cute, fun and we loved her so.

I went back to work and her Granny Molly looked after her initially, which was great. She loved having her, and Lynn loved being with her Nana. When she was about two, she went to playschool and loved it, as she enjoyed the company of the other children. She was a lovely little girl, very outgoing, but in a quiet sort of way, if that makes sense. She made friends easily, and had a few little pals on the road where we lived.

We lived in Clondalkin originally, but moved to Blanchardstown when Lynn was four, mainly because of the location of the school we had chosen for her which was in Glasnevin. We had originally put down a deposit on a house off the Navan Road, but as our solicitor had problems with the builder over right of way, we ended up pulling out of that, and found the house we actually love to this day. Although in the interim, it caused us a lot of problems and extra expense, and we were under a lot of stress at times, having to store our furniture and stay with family, it really was the right thing to do. That other house would not have been the right one for us at all.

Lynn started primary school in an Educate Together School, North Dublin National School Project in Glasnevin, one of only three of its type at that time. Friends' children attended the school, and we felt it the perfect one for her, even though it still meant travelling some distance. There was a private bus, run by a wonderful lady, which collected Lynn close to our home and took her to Glasnevin. I was working for a company in town at the time, and would leave her to the bus first. Lynn was about eight when the bus service finished up, and it was panic stations, wondering how we were going to manage as it was impossible to take her over to school ourselves. For once, I had a bright idea

– one of those rare eureka moments! I called the National Bus service at the time, and suggested they might run a bus on the route to Glasnevin, and within that, they could also bring service to other school children along the way. Even as I put down the phone after the first call, I thought how silly I was, and this was never going to happen. But, miracle of miracles, they went for it, and the headache subsided. I was very grateful to CIE. Remember, Lynn was only eight years old, but Lynn being Lynn was quite capable from that day onwards of heading around to the village (only three minutes from our home admittedly), and getting that bus herself, and same in reverse. She was always advanced and independent – a precious girl.

She loved the school and quickly made friends, with one special friend, Siobhán, who was to remain special to the end. She was a good student and liked her studies, but also got involved in the social aspects. Through the years, she had her birthday parties and went to many others as well. She spent a lot of time with Siobhán and her family in Malahide, with whom we were to become close friends. If Lynn wasn't in Malahide, Siobhán was with us in Blanchardstown.

Lynn joined a Drama Group when she was five, and again, she loved it, and especially loved the shows. The first big show, 'The Broadway Story', was in December of 1995, when she was nine, and we had Laura home from hospital for the longest time. It ran for a week and she was great and played many parts – it was so good for her to have that, having played such a back seat since her little sister was born. Otherwise, through Lynn's younger years, we went on holidays once a year and did all the things most families do

– nothing extraordinary, so Lynn's life was very ordinary, up to Laura's birth.

It was hard for Lynn knowing her little sister was sick, and during the almost seven months Laura was in Our Lady's Hospital, after two surgeries, she was very much left out, not through the fault of anyone, but just through the circumstances of our situation. I was later to remember the affect having a seriously ill child has on the other siblings also. Sometimes they are the forgotten ones, and it often goes unnoticed for obvious and understandable reasons. Lynn never complained though, and even at her tender age just got on with whatever each day brought. I often wonder, though, if she worried much more than she pretended, and although we were honest with her about Laura's condition, we did also try to protect her, especially when Laura was particularly poorly.

Eventually, though, in those early days when Laura came home from hospital, Lynn got to enjoy the little sister she waited so long for. She adored Laura, had such fun with her, played with her and showed her off to everyone. She taught her a lot of things too, in her short little life. I wish sometimes now that we had known the future – we probably would have gone to all the places and done all the things we wanted Laura to experience when she was better. But, of course, we were not to know her life was to be so short, as we actually did at the end of Lynn's life. They would both have done and seen many things they never did. But, that's the cards they were dealt I guess, and it wasn't to be for them.

Lynn was growing into a young lady also over those four years, and continued to do well in school and in her Drama, and went on holidays with friends and family, as we could not travel so much with Laura. Again, looking back, I'm sorry we didn't take a few chances and do some of the things we had planned for when she had her heart 'fixed', and all was well. Of course, we weren't to know that would never happen!

As related in Laura's story, the news of Lynn's diagnosis came as a horrible shock to us all. Even as our hearts were breaking at dear Laura's condition, we had to now help poor Lynn the best we could to deal with her illness. How we got through those days is a mystery to me. But what could you do? You just had to do your best and carry on. What was important was giving all possible support to our two girls.

Lynn's treatment started then in earnest. The only chemo she was sick on was the first one, and not too sick at that. Unfortunately, she had other side effects, the worst being a fungal infection on the lung, developed from the leukaemia treatment, for which she had to have further treatment. This, of course, meant more time spent in the hospital than would otherwise have been necessary.

She had a tough time for sure, poor darling, but was always so very positive. In fact, there was a joke with the nurses about her positivity. Every time they asked, 'How are you today, Lynn Mc Kenna?', she would always reply, 'Fine, thank you'. Eventually they started to ask a slightly different question which was, 'Is that good fine or bad fine?'

As she loved to sleep in her own bed, she pushed the Consultant and staff to free her to go home as often as possible. She also got to school, when she could, which was not very frequent that first year, but she truly loved school. I guess it was the normality of it all, and being with friends she loved and missed.

When her hair started to fall out, she had it shaved off, and I will always remember how very sad I felt, looking on, and thinking how very brave, forgetting perhaps that she really had no choice. In photos of that time she still managed to smile through it all. I just felt like crying and did, but not in front of her. She never wore a wig, but did wear a cap, and we used to look at caps regularly. Her hair would grow in between, but she looked gorgeous with or without it. She had lovely big blue eyes and beautiful eyebrows, and she didn't lose eyelashes or eyebrows, which was a definite plus.

As she continued treatment, Lorraine was not doing so well in James's hospital and sadly, she died on her 22nd birthday in November 1999 – about 10 weeks after our little Laura. Lynn attended her funeral and she shed some tears that day, first time I saw her really cry. It was all so very sad and so very awful. We could ask the question 'Why', but there are no answers, of course.

We came to Christmas, and Lynn was doing well enough, and was due to be out for the holiday, which was great. Again, I don't remember, but we must have done some shopping, one of her favourite pastimes. Certainly, as she deserved, she got some selection of presents, including a new computer, which the family clubbed together to get her. She was thrilled.

We were invited to my brother Maurice's for Christmas dinner, and Lynn was looking forward to my sister-in-law Marie's cooking. When she was younger, and Laura was still in hospital, she would often stay with Marie for a few hours, and they would so some baking. Her favourite subject was Home Economics, and I think it would have been catering college for her if things had been different. She also spent time with Ann, another friend of mine, who is in the catering industry. Ann would take her into where she worked in the Kings Inn, and she would support the catering staff, and learn some of the ropes of entertaining the powers that be there. She really loved it, and would be given a few pounds. Ann and staff would send her cards in hospital, and tell her to get well soon, and come back to them.

She also loved her food when she was feeling good, and still tried to eat even when she didn't feel great. When she was on steroids, she would eat rings around her, and got a fad for salmon. I remember asking her if she could change her fad to something a little less expensive – it was costing us a fortune. She never did!

Christmas day came, and unfortunately Lynn's mouth was sore from the treatment she was on at the time. However, we went for dinner, and she tried so hard to eat, but was really feeling more and more unwell as the day progressed – in quite a lot of pain, I suspect. We eventually made the decision to go to the hospital, as she needed some pain relief. I remember feeling so sorry for her and, if I'm honest, for us too. There were no patients on the ward, as they do their best to let all the children home for Christmas Day, so it was a really sad time. Lynn was given morphine and drifted off to sleep, at least now comfortable, I thought. The nurses were so good, and gave us a glass of wine, and tried to cheer us up a little. It is hard for them, too, being away from their families on that day, especially if they have young children themselves. That Christmas was so very hard anyhow, as the previous one had been so full of joy, fun and excitement, with Laura home and Santa coming, so in some ways it didn't make it any more difficult to be in the hospital.

The next few days were spent with Lynn recovering a little from the sore mouth, and trying to eat again. She was always so brave, rarely complained, and just got up and got on with it (as was the case with most of the sickest children – which always amazed me). Nearly all of the children were little ones, so it was often difficult for Lynn and for us, as most of the time, we had to share a room, and of course the little one would expect to look at 'Barney' and other cartoons, which were all favourites of Laura's. I remember feeling very worn out with it all, at times.

There was also a play room, but again, it was geared towards the little ones. Someone donated a little pool table, so on occasion, when there might be another teenager there, Lynn would go and play a game with them. She would also go and spend some time with the little ones and helpers, if she felt up to it, but I think it was hard for her, as it brought back memories of her little sister she was undoubtedly missing so much, although she didn't talk about her. She got on well with the staff, and loved the bit of banter. She liked them all, but did have her favourites. One of her favourites was Eileen, from Donegal, who would threaten Daniel O'Donnell on her from time to time. As you can imagine, he would not have been in Lynn's list of favourite artists, so they had some fun with that.

She had a great relationship with her Consultant, and always needed and wanted honesty and to be included in everything – even when the news wasn't pleasant. She was pretty mature from a very young age, so I guess this stood to her. She continued to have ups and downs, but eventually went into remission after her term of treatment finished around May 2000. There's a certain relief in that for sure, but it is far from being over, and somehow, you are nearly more worried and nervous then, because of the fear of relapse. Or maybe that was just me! I often think if she had stayed in remission, and lived, it would always be there in the back of your mind, and so you would never fully relax. However, as time would go on, the worry and concern would probably ease and perhaps fade? Again, we will never know.

During her treatment, the Courts Service where I had worked decided to do a fundraiser to raise funds for us to go on a holiday or use as we pleased. One of my work colleagues got the idea, and as her sister worked in the Gresham Hotel, a very wonderful and special night was held there. It was a professionally run Fashion Show, in which Lynn was excited to take part and had even gone along to rehearsals beforehand. Her friend Sibhy took part with her, and lots of friends and families attended. It was such a fun night and Lynn looked beautiful in her outfits – some of which she liked, and others not so much. It was in between treatments, and her hair had grown back somewhat, which was great. Little did I know then, that there would be many fundraisers ahead for me to attend and speak at for a very different reason.

Lynn was pretty exhausted after it, but elated too, and it is lovely to have the beautiful and now so poignant photos. The donation raised was about £4,500, and we decided to give something back to the Cardiac Department by giving funds to buy a small monitor that a heart child could have at home. It cost £2,500. The balance we spent on a holiday to Bonn in Germany to visit my brother James (whom Lynn was very close to), after she had completed her treatment protocol. We had a lovely time, staying in the apartment of a friend of James's, which was the most fabulous apartment imaginable.

Little did we know then that it would be the last holiday we would have together. I remember being very sad about Laura on that holiday, as while we were trying to concentrate on getting Lynn well again, and getting on with life, I missed her so much. My heart literally ached! I know Lynn and Brendan must also have had aching hearts too, but they never spoke of her, and then I didn't either. It sometimes seemed to me like she never really existed.

Later that summer, I remember, Lynn wanted to get her nose pierced and I was so against it, wondering, apart from anything else, how she would want to go through more pain involving needles. On a last visit to her Consultant, I brought up the piercing, hoping he would say a definite 'No.' Of course, he said he was not getting involved in a 'domestic' issue, but just to be sure to go to a reputable piercing shop, so I had no choice but to give in. I also remember finding the shop recommended and being horrified to find it was first and foremost a 'sex' shop, at the back of which was the piercing section.

Lynn's Uncle James was home on holiday with us, but he refused to come in and said he'd meet us later. I was mortified as we walked through the shop, and Lynn probably knew more about some of the stuff hanging about than I did. Then, when I saw the big hairy, tattooed, leather-clad piercer, I nearly collapsed, and I remember asking if the needle was absolutely sterile, as Lynn had leukaemia. Lynn immediately said, 'I *don't* have leukaemia', and I never made that mistake again, and of course she was right, at that point in time. I was also supposed to get my nose pierced, but even after watching Lynn get this huge, thick needle through her nose and not flinch, I still chickened out (too old anyway, I told them). Bit of a coward, I'm afraid! Lynn often slagged me over it, and rightly so, I suppose.

Lynn started third year in secondary that September and couldn't wait to get back to school, friends and 'normal' life. She enjoyed every moment of school, even the homework/study part, especially her favourite subject, Home Economics. She once made an apple crumble for her Aunty Irene's visit, and on noticing Laura eating slowly Irene asked her if she liked Lynn's desert. Laura, 3-years-old, said very diplomatically, 'Well, I likes it, but I don't likes it that much!' We all laughed, including the little 'madam'.

She was so happy to be 'well' again. I was still working away in the Estate Agents, and still enjoying it, and life became somewhat 'normal' again, except for the huge missing of Laura, by all of us, though I was probably the only one who talked of her. Lynn would often be with me when I did talk and cry, and maybe it was her way to deal with what was such terrible sadness for her.

During her illness, Lynn also joined Canteen, the teenage cancer group. She loved being part of that, and would often bring a friend to the meetings, events and trips. It is a wonderful support group for young people with cancer, who understand each other more than anyone else can. They have such fun and often make new friends for life. She also went to the Barretstown children's camp in Kildare, and spent many weekends at the wonderful facility, sometimes accompanied by friends, and on the ten day summer camp alone. She truly adored Barretstown, and made many friends from home and abroad (the summer camp brings in children from around Europe). She loved the activities, the freedom, being away from home and parents, hospitals and doctors –

though there were docs/nurses, continued treatment and a 'Med Shed', but not in your face. Again, it helped to share her illness with other young people who understood, and were going through the same, albeit each in their own individual ways. I think she would have stayed forever, if she could. The staff and *Caras* (Irish for friends) were amazing in the great work they do there, and we will always be grateful for the joy Barretstown brought to our daughter. A lot of kids who experience Barretstown return to work in a voluntary capacity as *Caras* themselves, and I truly think Lynn would have done just that. I too experienced the wonderful place, sometime later, and so truly understood why it had meant so much to Lynn. It meant a lot to me also, in dealing with the loss.

Lynn, still on maintenance, had to go for regular visits to check all was still in order, and mostly her Dad would go with her, or sometimes, both of us would. All continued well into the autumn and Lynn and I decided that we would go to London for a weekend break. As I mentioned before, she loved London, especially the West End shows, as she loved her own Drama group, which she still attended and hoped to do another big show, which was in the pipeline. I knew though, that she worried she would have to wear a wig, as her hair had not sufficiently grown yet. She was determined to do it though, and so looked forward to it. She continued to be well and her hair had grown beautifully, and she looked so pretty. We went off on our special little treat to London late November and stayed in a hotel right in the centre, which was basic but fine. We had a great time, and got to see three shows, including *The Lion King*, which we came across on the Saturday afternoon, and got into for a snip, but unfortunately had to stand. I remember noticing that Lynn was a little weak and asking if she might sit on the steps. I don't remember consciously thinking anything was wrong at that point, but maybe my mind just wouldn't allow me, because later I felt I had known then! We came back from London and back to normal life for another short while.

I can't say when, but Lynn went back for her check-up sometime early December. I always remember her and her Dad coming back in, and Lynn saying, 'it's back, I know it's back', and felt my heart sink, hoping against hope she was wrong. As it turned out, unfortunately, she was right, as we got a call from the Consultant to say the leukaemia was back (did it ever go?), and we now had to face the only option available, the thing we dreaded most, a bone marrow transplant.

We went into the hospital next morning and her Consultant looked at and spoke to Lynn directly and told her it was back, and they could give her some more very tough treatment, heading towards transplant, but it was up to her, if she would take it or leave it. She didn't even look at us sitting behind her, and didn't hesitate at all – just said she would take it. I remember asking him later what he would have done, had she said she wouldn't take it, and he said he knew her well enough to know she would say 'yes', but if not, it would have had to be discussed. He was right.

Siobhán's fifteenth birthday party was shortly after this, and Lynn couldn't wait to go and meet all the friends she knew through the years (especially the boys), and as it was fancy dress, she went as a devil, with big red horns. She had a great time and was always up for a bit of fun, wherever she could find it. She really did always try to have as normal as possible a life, while she could. She knew what lay ahead soon, and must have dreaded it, though she never said so.

Next leg of the journey, and the start of another very tough road for our beautiful, brave girl. What followed really was even more horrific than I ever imagined, and she had her head shaved, once again, least of her troubles! This treatment almost wiped her out, as I guess it's meant to do. Although I'm quite the coward, and would not want it really, I honestly wished so many times that it could be me. If only I could take it all away from her, but of course, it's the one thing no one else could do.

Christmas 2000 was not a pleasant one either, though, as always, Lynn made the best of it, and for the most part had a smile on her face and fun with staff. They had a dress up day, where the staff wore 'dogs' ears, and painted their faces to look like Dalmatians, and Lynn made 40 pairs of ears. Her Consultant said he wouldn't wear them, and Lynn told him in no uncertain terms that he would, and he did. She was home for Christmas Day, though wasn't so well. My brother James was staying with us, and she was delighted to have the company and an extra person in the house. She would have been well spoilt, rightly so, with lots of presents. I've often thought since then, why could she not have had just that one more Christmas in remission? She surely deserved it. One's faith, whatever that might be, really is pushed to the limits in situations like these.

Christmas came and went, and we were in the hospital more often than not, and again the treatment was so very tough. We had just come back from the hospital one evening, and Lynn was lying on the sofa, when Brendan called me from the kitchen where I was cooking, to look at Lynn (luckily he had just come back from the shop). I screamed as I saw her having a bad fit, and panicked. I called 999, and they sent an ambulance, and because of the time of day (6.00 pm), Lynn was brought to Blanchardstown Connolly Memorial Hospital, which we live beside. Brendan went in the ambulance and I followed in the car, shaking like a leaf. I don't know how I drove at all.

They had her inside in casualty, and we asked them to call Our Lady's, so they could be updated on her condition, before giving her any medication, as we were worried they might medicate her wrongly. She was still fitting, but not as badly, and while we couldn't understand what she was saying, apparently she could understand us, which is unusual for someone in a fit. She just couldn't speak clearly herself. She was taken to a room in I.C.U. for the night, with the fitting under control, though there were a few times she felt it start up again. We stayed with her until the early hours and then, because we lived so close, it was suggested we go home and come back early in the morning. She had a comfortable enough night, poor darling, and was so glad to see us, and looked forward to getting back to Our Lady's where, though strange to say, she felt more at home.

Back in Crumlin, more tests were done by the Neurology team and Lynn had to go have an MRI scan in Temple Street, and meanwhile she was put on further medication to control/stem the fits. She related the story of her 'crazy' Mum's antics when she took the original fit, and gave them a good laugh. She was also amazingly brave, as when she would feel the start of a fit (her little finger would start to tremble), she would say, 'No, I am not going to let this happen', and would bring it under control – she had great stamina and willpower.

46

She had her MRI scan, and I remember saying to her that by the time she was finished, she would have been in every hospital in Dublin, and at that point we didn't know how true that was to be – she still had a couple to go.

The various tests didn't bring answers, other than there was some sort of 'mass' discovered in her head (back of her brain, I think), and it was thought that it might be the cancer gone into the head, or something else. The next suggestion was that she be sent to Beaumont for surgery to see what might show. We couldn't believe she had to go through this now, on top of all she'd been through already. Meanwhile, the family were tested to find a match for her bone marrow transplant, but none were found. However, they had found several very good matches from their worldwide bank of donors, which was a bit of light at a very dark time. Lynn was still in and out of hospital, probably more in than out. She noted in her little diary that she so loved to sleep in her own bed, no matter what time it was that she got there, but I knew that anyway, and I guess it would be the same for any of us.

Her Consultant was anxious to have the brain surgery done as soon as possible, so he finally got the surgeon in Beaumont to operate on Saturday, March 3rd. The reason I remember this date so clearly is that it was my birthday the day before, which was when he told us. We had planned to go have a bite to eat, which Lynn was looking forward to, and when she was told this she was not at all happy.

However, we had to check into Beaumont late on the morning of my birthday, and the first thing Lynn asked the surgeon was could we go out that evening for her Mam's birthday, and she pretty much talked him into it. He told her not to be back too late. She was so happy to walk back out of that hospital, and we went to our own local Italian restaurant (which we often went to), and had a meal. Lynn wasn't eating very well, and really didn't eat much, but just wanted to be there, and wanted me to 'enjoy' my birthday. She knew she had to face having surgery on her brain early the next morning, and yet could think of me – how unselfish is that? She rang Dolores and asked her to come and join us for a coffee, which she did – I think she wanted us to have a bit of company on the day. We went back to Beaumont and I stayed with Lynn that night, dreading the morning, as I'm sure she was too, though she never voiced it – bravery again.

The surgery was scheduled for around 11.00 am, and Brendan came over to join us. We walked to the theatre with Lynn, and I remember thinking as she was taken away from us on that trolley that my heart would break, and that this was one of the hardest things we had to do in all we'd been through. Strangely, Lynn had always liked going to theatre and having the anaesthetic, and I always said to her that it took so long to go out of the system, that if she could do without it for some procedures, she should. She never took my advice – loved the peaceful sleep that anaesthetic brought, and who could blame her? Can't quite remember how long she was gone, but it seemed an eternity. Eventually, though, she was back in I.C.U. initially, and was brought to her own room later, I think. It was good to have our own room, as we had spent the night in a larger ward. She had quite a long opening in her head, as we found out later, which was obvious as she had very little hair – again. We stayed for about a week in Beaumont and it seemed the 'growth' (which had a very long medical name) in her head was caused by the horrific treatment trying to kill off the returned leukaemia, and this was found out through communication with medics in the States. The treatment kills off everything in the body and the immune system is so low that anything can happen. This is, of course, my simple understanding of the situation. We were so glad to be home again, though Lynn was back in Our Lady's once again, in and out, but this time round, more out than in.

Lynn's appetite was not so good at this stage, though she still loved her food and would try to eat, even when she really wasn't feeling hungry. Her fifteenth birthday was coming up on March 11th, and she just wanted to spend it with a few close friends, such as Siobhán and Ciara. She decided to go to her favourite local restaurant, Trentuno in Castleknock. We got her the latest runners in Schu in O' Connell Street, and were lucky to get her size. She loved all the latest gear, and like all teenagers didn't have a clue or care about cost. Anyway, what did it matter – she deserved it so.

Her birthday fell on a Sunday, and after she and the girls had had their meal in the restaurant, we had friends and family over later on. When I look back at the photos of that day, I see how sick and poorly Lynn looked, and it makes me so sad. Yet, as always, she put a smile on her face, when I'm sure she didn't feel like smiling. She enjoyed her time with friends and we had a cake for her too.

The evening after, myself, Lynn and Dolores went to collect a video from a friend's husband, who had prostate cancer and used an alternative diet from Mexico, and we wanted to have a look at it. On the way back, Lynn said she would love to go down to Trentuno again, and have some garlic mushrooms (her favourite), as she hadn't had them the day before on her birthday. Of course, we said okay.

We parked in the car park at the back and as we got out of the car, a hooded guy jumped out of another car and grabbed my bag from my shoulder, and got back into a car, which shot out to the main road. It was such a terrible fright, and I know Lynn was very shaken by it, but she put her arms around me to comfort me. I often wondered if it hastened her death, but this is probably another irrational thought, though the shock certainly did her no good. She never did get her mushrooms that night – poor angel! I remember thinking, 'why did this have to happen, on top of all we were going through?' Another question unanswered.

Back to Crumlin, and continued treatment, and her Consultant requested (I reckon pleaded) with St. Lukes to do the pre-transplant measuring etc., for Lynn. At that time, a lot of the children had to go to Scotland, and I think he knew we were going through enough (and I'm aware we weren't the only ones). They agreed thankfully, and we went over by taxi on a lovely Wednesday morning. I couldn't go into the rooms with Lynn, but eventually she was done, and while we waited for the taxi we had a cup of coffee, and I remember the memories of my Mum's time there, not too long before she died. Many moons before, when I was 20 and she only 50. Did I ever think then that I would be there with my 15-year-old daughter? We went out in the sunshine, and there was a swing there, which Lynn sat on, and I remember looking at her and thinking how much better she looked then than she had on her birthday a week or so previous. I had such hope she was going to be all right at that moment, a hope that was to be shattered within hours.

Back to Crumlin and Lynn was going to go finish a psychology test she had done the first half of the day before.

This is a test that's done before transplant, with another after. I never understood the reason, but I guess to see if there's a difference in brain levels, before and after. Lynn liked these kind of challenges, but before she got to head off, the Neurologist, who was due to come another time, arrived unexpectedly and got her to draw a man. Don't ask me why that drawing, as I have no idea! Then one of the nurses came to take bloods. I remember asking why she was taking more bloods, as she had taken some earlier, and she gave me a vague reason which I wanted to believe but somehow didn't. At that point, I just knew there was something wrong.

They also told Lynn she could go home for the night after all, though she was supposed to stay over, as she had a further test in the morning. She was so delighted to be getting home, she decided to leave the rest of the test, and asked if we could go to Brendan's sister for dinner, which Irene was delighted about. We headed to Ashbourne, and while she had been excited, she looked tired now, and didn't actually eat very much. I had phoned the hospital earlier to try to contact the Consultant, but couldn't get him, and it was suggested I try later. I had this awful sinking feeling in my stomach, one of utter gloom, and I think we both knew the news was not going to be good.

Back home late enough, and Brendan went up with Lynn to chat with her, as he often did, and I called the hospital again. I was told that the Consultant would call me back, and he did, to tell me the worst news I already knew, but so hoped I was wrong about. The leukaemia was back (never really went away, in my opinion), and Lynn was going to die – there was nothing else to be done. I cried and asked him how we would tell her, and he said, if we wished, he would do it in the morning. I told him I didn't want to go to the ward, so he said he would meet us at the end of the ramp. When Brendan came down, and Lynn was asleep, I told him and we just cried and cried. I don't think we slept at all. When I look back now, at that moment in time, I don't know how I didn't scream and scream and go completely mad.

We got up next morning and I remember hugging Lynn to me, and we could have told her, and would have, but for some reason, didn't. We headed over to Our Lady's, on what was to be our last journey there while Lynn was still in this world. The Consultant met us at the ramp, as arranged. I'm sure Lynn must have known there was something up, but she didn't say. I think she just knew, and was putting off the moment until she had to deal with it. We went up the ramp, which was usual, and I thought he was taking us to the ward after all. However, we turned right instead, and went to an office I didn't know was there. We sat down – Lynn, in front of him, with just Brendan and myself and a nurse, and he told our brave, beautiful Lynn, who had gone through so much already, that she was going to die (I'm crying hard, as I write this).

She just cried a little, then asked him how long had she got and what way would she die? He told her anything from two to eight weeks (which we all knew rarely happened – even Lynn), and her body would gradually wind down. I remember thinking, 'if you lie down there now, and die on the spot, I don't blame you', but of course our amazing girl just said okay. We got up to leave, to get on with the little bit of life she had left, whatever that might be. Her Consultant, being the lovely man he was, gave us all a hug and turned away crying himself. He called us a few times in the week Lynn was

Lynn (10) and Laura (6 months) taken before her first surgery.

Me, Lynn (8) and Laura, almost 2 months
– 17 February 1995.

Laura's first birthday on
ventilation in Our Lady's.

Lynn (9) and Laura (6 months) in the garden.

Me, Lynn and Laura – one of my favourite photos.

Lynn with Laura, finally home from hospital after seven months.

Lynn (4), Gillian (11), Lorraine (13). Lynn's first day at NDNSP, and Lorraine's fist day in second level, Coolmine Community School.

Laura in Skibereen, less than a month before she died. Her first and only holiday, and she was so happy.

Lynn (13) and Laura (4) in that fateful year, 1999.

A dear friend Hugh, and his dog Grizzy with Lynn and Laura – Grizzy was the same age as Laura and she loved him.

Brendan and Lynn, aged 2, in Menorca – her first holiday abroad.

Laura (4) sitting at the Christmas tree in 1998 – her fourth and last Christmas.

Lynn and Laura in the kitchen – Laura hugging 'Barney'.

Our beautiful 'Shirley Temple' – always smiling.

Lynn sitting at the Christmas tree in 1990,
when she was 4.

Lynn and me in Naas, on a day out.

Lynn's 8th birthday in McDonald's – great fun with her little group of special friends (1994).

Lynn and her best friend Siobhán in the school yard of NDNSP – they were about 6 years old.

Lynn and Grizzy, when she was 2 months old, as was Laura.

Lynn in her drama school rehearsing for *Broadway Story*.

Lynn (12) and Laura (3) on Lynn's Confirmation Day.

truly dying and he told me what an amazing daughter we had, which was lovely, though of course, we already knew that.

And as a very wise person once said, 'You can't do a lot about death, but you can do a lot about LIFE.'

I remember walking down that ramp for the last time, meeting a mother (whom we hadn't seen for some time) and her child going into the hospital, and chatting as if there was nothing wrong. I don't know what was said, but I think we must have gotten away quickly. I don't remember the drive home either, but clearly remember sitting in the kitchen, crying and saying to Lynn, 'How I wish I could take your place sweetheart', and her answer, 'Mam, it's okay, you must get on with your own life now'. Oh! What true courage! I hope I'll have even an ounce of it when my time comes.

Though we were together, it was probably one of the loneliest moments of all our three lives, as we were lost, and hopeless in our sad situation. We had no more crutches, no more hope, no one who could help save our darling Lynn.

Somehow, that same day, Dolores and Gillian (Mum and sister of Lorraine), managed to get tickets to a Westlife concert, who were playing in the Point Depot (now the 3 Arena). As it happened, there was another young girl from St. John's Ward going on her Make-a-Wish there that night. Lynn had helped her with her worry over losing her hair, and gave her a bit of courage at the start of her journey with leukaemia. I remember her enthusiasm about going (while they weren't necessarily her favourite group), and Dolores and I went along just to accompany them.

When the time came to go in, it turned out the escalator was broken, and we knew the climb up the stairs would have been a lot for Lynn. One of the security men, who was extremely kind, brought her and Gillian up in a private lift, which we were really grateful for. I did try to arrange for Lynn to meet the lads, but as it turned out that was for another time, and for more than just a 'meet and greet'.

Dolores and I had a drink, and talked about what lay ahead, while the girls enjoyed the concert. A very surreal conversation! I remember thinking later about how Lynn must really have felt that night. I shiver when I think that she was singing and dancing, most likely the only person in that huge stadium, who actually knew she would soon die. How did she do it – again, courage beyond belief! Brendan collected us and we must have all somehow slept that night, through sheer physical and mental exhaustion. I've no clear memory either way.

Friday morning dawned and Lynn decided she wanted to get false nails. It wasn't so popular then, but we manaaged to find a nail salon. Dolores took her there, and she and Lynn later recalled that the staff were not the friendliest. When the nails were complete, it was suggested to Lynn that she make an appointment to return in two weeks for a 'fill'. Lynn replied, 'Ah! You're okay, I'll leave it for now'. As Lynn didn't suffer fools gladly, and had a wicked sense of humour, I think it was the measure of her, given the cool atmosphere, that she didn't add, 'Sure I'll probably be dead by then'. But Lynn was very caring and would not want to hurt!

I can't recall what we did the rest of that day (certainly went out to eat, I would wager), or the following day, but on Sunday there was a wonderful surprise, which Brendan knew about, but Lynn and I didn't.

We knew that Siobhán's parent's, Phil and Con, were taking us to lunch in Cruzzo's in Malahide, and we knew it was a lovely, if quite upmarket restaurant, so really were looking forward to it. However, as we were almost ready, and Brendan was shouting at us to hurry up, Lynn looked out the window of Laura's bedroom, and said, 'Mam, there's a stretch limo outside the drive, and Phil and Siobhán are getting out'. I couldn't believe it, and some friends, who had just left the house a little earlier, had also come back (Brendan had told them), and we went outside to a celebration of champagne and chocolates. I'm sure our neighbours were wondering what was going on. It was so exciting and Lynn was thrilled.

We had a great day, strange and all as that may seem. The sun shone and we got to Malahide in our limo, and Siobhán's Dad, brother, aunt, uncle and cousins, whom we often socialised with, were waiting in the restaurant. We had a delicious lunch and Lynn ate pretty well and looked pretty good too, for someone who was dying. We had a few hours at the restaurant and then Siobhán and Lynn decided they would take the limo (which was available for the day) up to Siobhán's house to spend some time together, while the rest of us went for a drink.

I often wondered what they talked about, if they discussed Lynn's death and said their 'goodbyes'. I just don't know. I have a feeling they did though, as it was all so open. I don't remember much more of that day really. We spent a little time back at the house, and I think the limo left us home and we probably went to bed exhausted. I know Lynn slept with me for the rest of her little life – a comfort of sorts for us both, I guess.

Our next venture was to Dromoland Castle for Lynn's Make-a-Wish. We had only begun to plan it before her planned bone marrow transplant, but then knew she hadn't got much time so, needless to say, it wasn't her first wish. That was to meet Robbie Williams, whom she fancied madly – she always seemed to go for the wild ones! I wanted her to meet Michael Barrymore, who was a big celeb at the time, as I fancied him (he hadn't come out as being gay then) though he was quite wild too, so we had that in common in the men we liked. Of course, Lynn just laughed and asked whose wish this really was? Anyway, she was quite happy and really excited to go to Dromoland, which at the time was only for the wealthy – poor people like us didn't go to expensive places like that, so it was going to be a real treat. We will always be grateful to the Make-a-Wish group. They really do bring such happiness to sick children's lives, even, as in our case, when there is no hope.

We were flying from Dublin airport to Shannon, and Lynn thought it was only her Dad and Dolores coming with us, but we had secretly planned for Gillian and Siobhán to come too, so they had to go to the airport separately and wait until the last minute to go to gate. It must have been a twist of fate, but when we went through to duty free, the airport was particularly quiet, and Westlife, who were flying in a private plane to Manchester for the next leg of their tour, were just wandering around. Lynn got their autographs, and had photos taken with them, and couldn't believe her luck (little did she or they know that she would be with them in Manchester in the following few days). It was a fantastic surprise for her and she was just chuffed. We headed down to our gate then, and let Gill and Sibhy know it was okay to come down. They really surprised Lynn and she was so happy to see them, telling them of her encounter with Westlife, of which they were very jealous, especially Gill, as she fancied

Shane hugely. Again, though, she wasn't to know (as none of us did) at that point the great surprise which still lay ahead. I think she also was really glad she wasn't stuck with us old foggeys only, and who could blame her?

We arrived in Shannon, having had lots of fun, banter and laughter on the flight, and had a people carrier waiting for us. I drove, and felt a bit nervous, but soon got used to it, and somehow we found our way to Dromoland Castle without too much trouble. Gill and Siobhán were originally staying in another hotel, close by, but on our second night, they stayed with us.

I'll always remember Lynn's words as we walked into our suite, as Gill videoed it all. She said her whole house could fit into this space – a slight exaggeration, but it was quite sizeable. It was pure luxury and we settled in very well, got comfy and just relaxed awhile. There was a bottle of Meade, and although I don't normally drink whiskey or anything in that line, it was delicious, and so we enjoyed a glass or two. We later showered and dressed for dinner. We went all out, and the photo of us dressed up is such a poignant one, and Lynn looked so lovely. Would have been hard to tell she was dying, for sure.

We headed down for dinner, which was delicious, and Lynn was eating pretty well. We ate and drank and laughed, and probably looked like reprobates, amidst the sedate Americans and quiet affluent clientele. There was a girl singing and playing the harp, and for some reason the girls found it so funny, especially Lynn, and it was to lead to her eventually letting us know, as she made her funeral arrangements, that she did not want a harp playing, but more about that later.

I remember at one stage, as Gill was filming and Brendan taking photos, looking across at Lynn, and thinking to myself, 'what are you really thinking, my brave darling, and how have you got the strength to do what you're doing, knowing you are dying, at the tender age of fifteen'. I look at that photo often, and still remember my thoughts, still wonder at her courage, and always will.

Later, we went into the bar as the girls wandered around, having their own fun. I remember noticing a lady in the dining room earlier and there she was in the bar. She stood out, as she was unusual, in her long cloak, and we thought she might have been the owner or one of them. She eventually came over to us, and said she was delighted to see how happy our table was and the fun and laughter we were having. I told her our daughter was dying, and without flinching she said she knew. It was strange. She gave us her card, and as it turned out she was a preacher of some sort and lived in New York. I did write to her the following year, but never heard back. I wondered if perhaps she had died in the 9/11 attack. We'll never know of course, but if so, I thought she may well have met Lynn again, and Laura too.

We three adults stayed in the bar, had a few more drinks, while the girls wandered around the hotel, got into mischief, and though they could not possibly have been hungry again, when we got back to the suite they had ordered the biggest plate of sandwiches I ever saw. A very delicious looking mixture, half of which weren't eaten. I suppose they wanted to have a childish picnic and that's just what they did.

We slept really well and it was all so cosy. The bed could fit about five people, literally. Lynn got a lovely surprise, when she got a call from our friend from Our Lady's Hospital, to say she would be going to Manchester to see Westlife in the next few days. She was over the moon, and Gill is filming her, as she is mouthing the words, 'I'm going to see Westlife', which was very poignant for us to see later, and lovely to have now and always.

Up bright and early the next morning and we headed off to Bunratty Village and did some sightseeing in that beautiful place, with nice weather, which was a bonus of course. Can't remember much else, but think we went back, had lunch and rested a while, as we were booked into the banquet in Bunratty that night, and really looked forward to that. We all got into the 'glad rags' again, and headed on our journey. It was a really fun night, with Gillian filming the evening, and again lovely to have that DVD to look back at, though I don't do it often. Lynn had such fun, and it was a great night – a night to remember always. We got back quite late, all exhausted, us adults quite merry, so slept well. Up next morning, enjoyed a lovely last breakfast in Dromoland, feeling it unlikely we would ever darken the doors here again, and got ready to head for home.

The girls went off to have a final wander around and of course a bit of fun by taking a few items off the housekeepers trolleys – said they felt we were well paying for them, so didn't feel at all bad. We said our goodbyes to Dromoland, and headed for the airport. Left our car back and got our flight home. End of another little adventure in Lynn's all too short life.

Again, don't remember much else over the next day or so, as we were busy getting ready for Manchester. Lynn was still doing really well, and looked better than she had for awhile – very strange, considering she was dying. She couldn't wait to head off on her next adventure, and was delighted that Dolores and Gill were coming too. The flight out was fun and we were met by a chauffeur with a lovely big black car. He drove us to our hotel – a beautiful country house hotel on the outskirts of Manchester. It was pretty luxurious and we settled in well. The driver brought us on a tour – Old Trafford, Manchester United grounds, Coronation Street set etc., and then on to the Trafford Shopping Centre, which was enormous. Lynn loved shopping, so she was in her element. I don't think she actually bought anything – I guess she knew there wasn't much point really!

Back to the hotel and had some lunch, relaxed and got ready to head to the concert. She was so excited about meeting the lads, but little did any of us know what a great surprise lay ahead. We had been told whom to contact when we arrived, and it turned out to be a lovely young girl who brought us away from the others waiting to meet and greet. Turned out, we went down to the lads' private dining area, could have what we wished to eat and drink and relax. It was a lovely, cosy area, lit up with candles. Some of the lads were there, in particular Shane, Gillian's 'crush'. I watched Lynn watching Gill, and I really think she was so glad to see Gill happy (as she knew how sad she was, at the loss of Lorraine – just as Lynn was at the loss of Laura).

We were then brought up to the boys' dressing room, and sat down with them all – it seemed so unreal and even to us oldies, so exciting. I will always remember how kind they all were. Nicky made sure Brendan, Dolores and I had a drink, and he stayed chatting with us, saying at one point that it was hard to believe Lynn was actually dying. He was so very nice and caring. The other lads had brought Lynn and Gill (with Kerry Katona and friend) backstage and showed them all the props, their outfits for the night and they apparently had amazing fun. It is something Gill remembers to this day, especially spending time with Shane, whom she always said she would marry one day. He did marry a 'Gillian', but sadly, not our Gill. When they came back to the dressing room, we all sat and chatted, laughed, and then the lads said they had better get ready for their concert. Before we left, we took some photos and Lynn said to Nicky that he'd better say something to her from the stage, and he said he'd do more than that.

We were then brought up to a private suite, which turned out to be Kerry Katona's, and she was there with a friend and her foster parents, who had another foster child, a young boy, with them. Lynn had the choice to stay in front of the stage with Gill, which she initially chose, but just before the boys came on, she decided to come on up to the suite. Turned out the escalator was broken and they had to climb the stairs, which Gill said nearly killed her, never mind Lynn. It must have taken so much out of her – don't know how she did it. We were surprised, but delighted to see her, as she could sit and relax and had a fabulous view of the stage. She, Brendan and Gill sat outside, and Dolores and I inside. It was an amazing view we had of the enormous stadium, and great having our own space – so much room.

I was really glad Lynn had made the choice to come up, as I was a bit worried about her standing and being in the crowd, though she would have had a special place in front of the stage. The concert started and the lads were brilliant – stage, lighting and props were amazing. The third song in, and Nicky announced that this was for Lynn, a special friend from Ireland, and the song was 'Swear It Again'. Dolores and I were crying and I remember thinking, if only this were for a very different reason, and not because Lynn was dying. Gill told us that they were all crying too, though Brendan would never admit it, and Lynn did it very quietly. It was all so sad and yet so exciting for Lynn and for us all, I guess. We had a bit of a job finding the driver after the concert ended, and were very tired by the time we arrived back at the hotel, so I think we all slept well that night. We had a lovely breakfast next morning and again, memory fails me, as to what else we did, before heading back to Dublin. I do remember in the airport that Lynn was a little weak, and we had to walk a distance to board. We wanted her to have a wheelchair, but she refused point blank.

We will always be so grateful to our friend and all involved in organising and sending us on that wonderful trip to Manchester, and hope you all know how much it meant to all, especially Lynn. We, her parents, hold the memories dear to our hearts forever.

Being the eternal optimist, Lynn then wanted us to go to Bonn in Germany, to visit her Uncle James, who still lived and worked there. We actually had to beg her to give us a break, as we were all exhausted. She loved James and got on really well with him, and as mentioned before we had gone to stay with him on a few occasions (including during her remission). She and I had also gone to Bonn, and driven to Paris with him, to stay with a friend, before she got sick.

I'm so glad she at least did get to see a couple of places outside Ireland, we got to go to London and that we had some time for just us girls together. Anyway, I think she knew she truly would not be able for it, but just wanted to fit in all she could. James did come home to see her (can't recall which weekend it was), and I remember the sadness of the goodbye, as of course they both knew that the next time James was home would be for her funeral, and there was nothing that could change that except perhaps a miracle, and they don't happen too often!

In her last week, as her Consultant had told her, her body started to wind down and she got weaker each day. She still tried to eat – always did love her food – and she did eat pretty well, for someone so close to death. Family and friends were wonderful and such a great help to us all, with moral support and practical things, like making dinners, getting groceries etc. In particular, Siobhán and her family came quite a lot, and I know how much this meant to Lynn. Looking back, it is such a surreal time, and almost impossible to explain, even to myself. I knew Lynn was close to death and leaving us, and yet we carried on with everyday life, albeit not in a normal way. It is really hard to even understand how we did it.

A few days before she died, she was acting a little strange, and I was hoping she was not going to lose her mind, and not know us – I just did not want to remember her that way. My friend Carol and her daughter Ciara, Lynn's friend, came around, and again, so supportive with practical things, and having Ciara make some fun with her. On this particular day, she was saying funny things – just a little strange. She wanted Dolores to get some sweets, cakes and drinks, and thought we could have a little party – a bit like a little girl. Dolores could imagine all the crumbs and mess in our bed, and was worrying how I'd react, given how fussy I was. Anyway, the party (which I truly wouldn't have minded, of course) didn't materialise in the end. However, Lynn decided she would love some chips, and as she was eating them I noticed she was again acting strange, and kept dropping them. Turned out she then went into a fit, and of course, as always, I screamed and Dolores, who kept calm, administered the medication we had been given in case this should happen. She was fine after that, and back to herself, and (selfishly, I suppose), I was so glad the strangeness had gone. We had been told she might fit or bleed towards the end, and it was quite scary to even think about this. As it happened, this particular fit was the only occurrence, as I could not bear to even contemplate her having to return to Our Lady's.

A close friend had organised for Ronan Keating to surprise call her, but we didn't quite know when. About three days before she died, her mobile rang around 10.00 am, and as it happened, Dolores, Brendan and I were all in the bedroom. We knew by her face that she didn't know who it was, so we guessed it was Ronan, and as she spoke to him, she mouthed, 'it's Ronan Keating', and she chatted for quite a while. When the call was over, she told us he was calling from London, and was there to release his latest single 'Loving each day, as if it's your last' – how poignant. He asked her if she had heard it, and then said he hoped to meet her on Friday, as he knew we had been invited to the Mansion House, to an event to do with his own charity. As it turned out, his Mam's close friend, who was a friend of Siobhán's family also, was at Lynn's funeral on the Friday morning and at the event in the afternoon, and Ronan did ask her how Lynn was, which I thought was so nice. She was so excited that he had phoned her, and of course she was frantically texting friends, saying, 'guess who just called me from London?' Again, it was such a lovely treat for her at the end of her life, and we'll always be grateful to Ronan, and our friend who arranged it all.

We were to have another wonderful surprise on Easter Saturday morning. Mary McAleese, our ex-President, sent Lynn and us a beautiful Easter plant and an even more wonderful hand-written card, with words which were so meaningful. She was so honoured and thrilled, as we were, and we will treasure that card for ever, and kept a photo of the long since dead plant. I think that was Lynn's idea, as she knew that, like her, it would not have too long to live.

In those last few days she still managed to write her 'will', and thought about who she wanted to leave what to – things that meant something to each person. She also wrote the poem 'Lynn's Dreams', which showed her amazing courage and acceptance of her fate. She arranged her funeral. She wanted a white coffin, her watch, so she could tell the time, a torch, so she could see, her diaries so I couldn't read them, photos of Laura and Lorraine, and some letters, written to her in her last weeks.

She had our young priest, Kieran, whom she knew well and was so fond of, call over a few times too, in that last week, and we wondered what she chatted about. I did ask him later, and without breaking any confidences, he said her huge concern was for Brendan and myself, and how we would survive without her and Laura. She knew how broken-hearted we already were, as she was also, without Laura, and how it would be so much worse now. Still thinking of us, in her dying days – brave sweetheart.

In the last few days, she grew weaker and weaker. I had slept in the bed with her up until then, while Dolores slept in Laura's bed and Brendan in Lynn's, but now, I slept on a mattress on the floor, as she needed the space. One of the days we washed her and changed the bed, and put her on a fold up bed on the landing while we did this, and she said, 'Thanks for doing this Mam, I feel much fresher'. I feel so sad when I think of this, my beautiful darling, dying, and she thanks me for a simple thing! She was just so sweet and so good – I love her so. She still managed to get up to go to the loo, though there was not much left, she was quite heavy (really dead weight, I guess) and hard to manage – so very weak, poor darling.

On Wednesday morning, the 18th, Lynn said she was feeling a little pain, and was spitting up some black stuff – really so very weak and frail. The one thing she did wish was that she would not have pain, and so we phoned the nurse from Our Lady's Hospice, who said she would try to get to us for 1.00 pm – this was at about 11.00 am. We called our own GP, who was so lovely and came straight away. He administered some morphine and Lynn drifted off to sleep. She was comfortable and in no pain.

The nurse came around 1.00 pm or so and set up some more morphine. The day went on and Lynn remained asleep and people came and went, to say their 'goodbyes', as we knew time was short now. Nurse came again around 6.00 pm, and said she would possibly linger at least until the next day, and talked to us for a while, and then left. There was only Dolores and Brendan's sister Irene in the house, and we sat with Lynn again, lost in our own thoughts and sadness. I remember hoping that just as on the day of her birth, that on the day of her death there would only be Brendan and me.

A few minutes later, Brendan could feel her pulse weakening, and at 6.40 Lynn took her last breath. I remember she seemed to take another breath (which apparently happens), and I irrationally thought we had a miracle and she was going to live, after all. Of course, I knew she had gone. I got my wish anyhow, and just like the day she came into the world, so we were the only ones with her when she left the world – 15 years old – our second baby gone. The contrast of feelings of the joy of her birth and the devastation of her death, worlds apart. It was all so empty, so lonely – so utterly terrible. At least, she got one of her last dying wishes, and died peacefully at home.

We laid her out in our bed, and when the undertakers had embalmed her, Gillian did her makeup, as she had wished. She had chosen the clothes she wanted to wear: a top with an angel on the back – a gift from her Auntie Angie – jeans and the runners she had gotten on her birthday five weeks before. Dolores had said to her, 'You're not taking the good runners', and she said, 'Sorry Dolores, but I am'. She was so generous in all she gave to others, but she wasn't giving away the expensive runners – who could blame her?

She looked strangely beautiful and serene, even in death. We put the things she had requested in the coffin with her. We kept her with us for two days, which turned out in time to be such a comfort to us. Part of you never wants to let go at all, but of course you have to, though it's so hard. Family and friends came to see her, and some of her friends especially found it so hard. Young people, with their lives ahead, some of whom had never experienced any death yet, and one or two who did, sadly. I felt so very sorry for them.

We had the funeral on the Friday, April 20, another beautiful, sunny day. It was such a huge ordeal to close that coffin, and kiss our darling for the last time – it makes me feel so sick and sad to think of it now. It's horrific to have our two girls go – no understanding of it really. Why were they taken away – so young and vibrant? How were we going to live our lives without the beautiful girls who made it all worthwhile?

Lynn had chosen where she wanted to be buried – in a little country churchyard (I don't really like the words 'graveyard' or 'cemetery'), which is in the middle of the beautiful little village of Castleknock, where Lorraine was buried. One of her other last wishes was to have Laura brought and laid beside her, so we knew we would be granting that wish – only way it could ever be. As it turned out too, she was buried one grave away from Lorraine, which I know she would have wished for, but couldn't have chosen. That also is a comfort of sorts.

The mass was beautiful, and Lynn's Drama teacher sang and played the music, which was truly lovely. Lynn did say she didn't want the harp to be played, but I'm afraid it was. I had to laugh, though, as I could just hear her say, 'thought I told you I didn't want that'. As mentioned previously, when we were in Dromoland Castle, Lynn and her friends found the harpist funny every time she would play and sing in her 'soprano' voice. It was just a giddy thing for them, but they had such fun with it. It always brings a smile to my face and a sadness to my heart whenever I hear a harpist play.

Our priest Kieran, a close friend, spoke so amazingly (as he always did – part of what Lynn liked about him). He even said he wondered what kind of bastard God could let this happen, and I remember being shocked, mainly because my old and very special Aunt Babs, now sadly gone also, was somewhere behind, and I thought she'd be horrified, being religious, as women of her age were. However, I think even she probably agreed with him.

Lynn had requested that my brother James or Gillian read the poem she had written 12 days before she died, so Gill read it, and James read one of his own, which I know she would have loved. At the graveyard, we had 'Flying without Wings' played – one of Lynn's favourites. It was a terribly, terribly sad day – our two precious children gone from our lives forever more in this world. It is truly impossible to explain how it feels, and only those who have experienced the loss of their child can possibly understand. The birth of one's child brings greatest joy in the world, I think most would agree, and so, the greatest loss and sadness in the world, has to be the loss of one's child. Not to take away from other losses though – all truly sad.

I don't remember much of the day after that, just know we had family and friends around and I guess that was probably good – a little distraction. Although when your child or children have been ill, and you know the worst may well happen and they might die, you probably actually do some of your grieving along the way, and perhaps it does help, but there is a hell of a lot more grieving still to come. I think any parent losing a child truly grieves for the rest of their lives – there is no real respite from that. It is in the days and weeks afterwards, when everyone, understandably, has gone away, that the total numbness starts to wear off a little, and the stark reality of the loss hits home. However, it is actually months and really years down the road before the huge enormity of the loss truly hits home. One of the things that I remember vividly is how quiet the house was – how very empty, and yet, I also felt the girls' presence in a strange sort of way. In one small diary Lynn did not take with her, she had written after Laura had died about how quiet and silent the house was now, and it broke my heart to read it, as she had never spoken of it.

People ask, even all these years later, 'how do you go on?' and my answer is always the same, 'how could I not?' There are actually only two choices – you do, or you don't, and the 'don't' would mean only one thing – committing suicide – not an option for me, but I can understand why it might be for some. I would never knock or judge anyone on that road, and in a strange way I think it is a brave act, and generally those people are in a very bad place mentally. Of course, it is totally devastating and horrendous for those left behind. In my case, however, I saw my girls fight their illnesses so hard for their short lives. They wanted so hugely to live, loved life with all their hearts and souls, but still dealt with life and death in an amazingly courageous way, given their tender years. How could I possibly kick life in the face, and not try to make the best of it, and perhaps try to help others too? Even trying then to give something back, if for no other reason than the fact I'm so lucky to have my own health to date – something no money can buy, and something I treasure greatly each and every day.

What gives me strength and courage to carry on is the bravery and acceptance of my two amazing girls. Laura in her own little way, almost always had a smile on her mischievous little face, was full of fun and loved every minute of her short life, and was so brave, despite all she went through, almost like she somehow knew her life would be short. She never got to do very much, but she was loved so much and brought great joy and happiness to her Dad, Lynn and me, and of course our extended family and friends. She did, without doubt, suffer a lot in her four and a half years, but I think she also experienced great happiness too – at least, I hope so.

Lynn was brave, courageous and accepting, in the most amazing way, despite her tender years. I'm so grateful for the many more years I had with her, and for all the things we shared, and the places we got to travel to together. In her last few days, she and I, at her request, shared little secrets no one else knew, and that was and remains so very special to me. She and Laura are my heroes, why I carry on, and try to live life to the full, as I wish they could have done, and what Lynn told me I must do. It is though, I admit, often easier to say and think this than to actually do it, but thank God and my girls, so far, I am doing okay.

I don't know what Lynn would have done or how her life would be now. I remember she and her friend Siobhán talking when they were about eight or nine, about what they wanted to be when they grew up, and how they would both go to Trinity College. Siobhán said she wanted to be a teacher, like her Mam, and Lynn said she wanted to be a hairdresser! I know her favourite subject was Home Economics, and she was pretty good at that, and I think catering is the area she may have studied and worked in. Who knows, maybe she would have her own restaurant by now, and be rich and famous! The unanswered and unaswerable questions!

On the following page is the poem Lynn wrote twelve days before she died.

Lynn's Dreams

I wish I could learn,
like everyone else.
I wish I could swim, jump and run,
I wish different cards could have been dealt
I wish it could be like old fun.

I wish I could grow and learn about life,
I wish I could feel well again.
I wish that there was an end to the strife,
And a new beginning instead.

But destiny's come and it's drawing me near,
And I know my two ANGELS are there.
With them I will have no reason for fear,
In their warm embrace and their care.

By Lynn McKenna, 6 April 2001

5

Life After Death

'Universal truth about death –
life goes on afterwards.'

After my girls had gone, probably without even thinking consciously about it at that time, I knew I had to try to find a reason to carry on. When you're alive, well and breathing, you don't consciously think you need a reason to live, but when your body and mind reel from the shock of such loss, you actually, without even realising it, have to push yourself to carry on. The emotions of your heart are shattered beyond belief, and you struggle to keep it beating.

It has been suggested to me on more than one occasion that I must have been tempted to pull the duvet over my head, and never again surface, and that I would not be blamed if I did just that. I guess I am lucky that I never actually did feel like doing that, though I would be less than honest if I said I didn't find it hard to face the day sometimes, and that is not just in the early days, but forever. It may seem to many that I am always positive and upbeat, but believe me, it is often easier said than done, and appearances truly can be deceptive. However, I always feel my girls around me, and truly feel they help guide and give me strength and courage to carry on somehow, even on the gloomiest of days.

I cried waterfalls of tears in those early days. I cried with the physical pain of missing them, not seeing, hearing or touching them – my heart was really 'broken'. I missed the word 'Mammy'. I missed the buzz of having a teenager and a cute little girl in the house. I missed that cute little girl's arms around my neck, and the unconditional hugs of love. The words 'I love you Mammy', uttered so constantly in the last four years, and years before, by Lynn, when she was little. I missed the noise, the hustle and bustle of life with two girls in the house. I hated the silence that surrounded and haunted me. I even missed the hospital and caring for them. I missed everything about my beautiful girls. It was a feeling of total unreality, and desolation. Yet somehow, I got up and got through each day, and I suppose again, without even consciously thinking it, took one day at a time.

I knew I needed to do something, if not work then what? I did try to return to work, but somehow, couldn't do it. I finally decided to go back to 'school'. There is a County Dublin VEC Adult Education Centre less than five minutes from my home, and I went there to do Leaving Certificate English, and the ECDL course in computers. I love English, and only had a slight grasp of computers, and unfortunately, not much has changed there! I suppose it's an 'age' thing, and I imagine my girls laughing loudly at just how averse I am to modern technology! Others probably just think I'm thick, and feel sorry for me, but I don't think I'm going to change on that front now.

I really enjoyed my time back at school – the tutors and staff were lovely, and I met some other interesting and very nice 'mature' students, some of whom became good friends, and one of whom I had grown up with. I very much enjoyed studying again, even doing the old homework! I think it's true to say that, as an adult, you make your own choice to study, and are also treated in an adult way, which actually makes it more enjoyable and interesting, rather than a boring and often unloved chore which had to be suffered. Not every young person feels that way, but I think most do, at some point or other in the early years of 'no choice'.

As I had never actually sat the Leaving Certificate, being able to get my 'good' job without it, I did the English L.C. exam that year and got an A1, which I felt very proud of. I did it partly for Lynn, as she would have been doing her Leaving Cert then too, and I think she might have done as well, if not even better. She was pretty good at English studies too.

Strangely, I eventually ended up working in my Adult Education Centre. I was offered a job in the Administration area, as secretary on reception, which is the type of area I was used to working in. So I decided to take it up, not realising at that point what else I was about to take on, and how my life would change so much. I loved working there, liaising with staff, tutors, students and the public, and because I am a 'people' person, and quite sociable, it was the perfect job for me. I was with the 'office' for about five years, most of which I was also running the LauraLynn Foundation. To say I worked 12 hour days then is probably an understatement, but that's how it was, and perhaps part of what helped me survive as well as I did.

The other thing I did was to volunteer in the local primary school, where Laura would have gone. I helped out once a week in a particular class with the little ones. I loved that, as I love children so much anyhow, though when I look back, I wonder how I managed it, as it must have been difficult picturing Laura there. Maybe I had to prove something to myself! I stayed there for a year or so, and like to think I made a small difference to the beautiful and precious little ones in that time.

I guess I did lots of bits and pieces, and then founded LauraLynn, while also holding down my part-time job, which left me very little time to dwell. I remember many times wondering 'WHY'? I think all of us at one point or another in our lives, and for various reasons, must surely ask that question, when bad and sad things happen. There are no answers, at least not that I can find. So, whatever our circumstance, where death plays a part especially, we can do nothing to change what is. We simply have to learn to live with it, and hopefully do our best to survive and carry on. Live a different life, but missing that special person on every occasion, and every day really. It's hard for anyone with any loss, but especially hard when it's your child.

LauraLynn and all it entails takes up most of my life, and probably will, for as long as I live, and I guess that can only be good. The magic of life, and the strength of the human spirit, without doubt, helps me carry on too. What also helps me greatly though, is the fact that I know my girls would be very unhappy if I did not make the best of a life cut short for them. I love life and people and the wonder of the world, for all its faults. Each day I have my health is a bonus, and I am truly grateful for that, especially as I grow older and the years pass so quickly. In the 'Departure Lounge' now, so time is of the essence.

I must say too, though, that for all that I do hope there's somewhere nice after this life, and how I have repeated many times in this book that I feel my girls are truly in paradise, I question deeply about 'Life after Death'. If I'm totally honest, I have to admit it is intriguing and a great mystery, and I really don't think any of us knows the truth of it. We just have to hope!

6

LauraLynn House

'It's not how long you live that matters,
it's what you do with the life you have.'

I can't remember the day that the idea of the need for a Children's Hospice came into my head – just that it did sometime early in 2002. I spoke to a close friend about it, and she thought it wonderful and encouraged me, saying she would love to help me with the idea. As things turned out though, she and her husband would shortly foster three beautiful children, to whom they are the most wonderful parents in the world, so that put paid to her support being available to me, but it wasn't to stop me, as time has proved.

As it happened, I was also approached at that time to take part in a documentary on Our Lady's Hospital, little knowing that it would be the first of many times I would appear on TV and be involved with the media. If someone had told me then the things I would eventually come to do, I would never have believed it, and would have said they were crazy. I would always have been the one hiding at the back of the room, behind the crowd, quite a shy person. Though I doubt anyone believes it now, I still am that shy person to a huge degree, and am still much more comfortable at the back of the room!

Anyway, that documentary was to lead to the 'real' start of the LauraLynn Foundation. After the program, I was approached by the journalist who was the family correspondent at the *Irish Times* then. She had seen the program, and wished to do an article on my sad story. Also, on hearing that I had plans to set up a charity to build a Children's Hospice, she insisted on including my address so that people could donate. Technology, besides my aversion to it, really wasn't such a viable option for most, in those days. Snail mail was still very much in vogue.

So in a way, the charity pretty much started itself off (or perhaps that journalist should take the credit!). No sooner was the article published than the cheques started to pour in my letterbox, and I remember being a little scared, as I had not officially set up LauraLynn, or even knew how to go about it. I thought, though, that either I do this now or I send back those cheques and forget about it all.

Of course, as history shows, I did the former, and very glad I did. Having said that, it's probably best that we can't predict the future because if I'd known just what was ahead, the hard work and long hours involved, I might have run a million miles away! I don't really mean that, of course – as I've said already, it is now such a wonderful joy to see the special care and comfort being brought to precious little ones and their families at LauraLynn House.

The year was 2002, and it was the start of a long and wonderful road, full of mixed emotions along the way. There has been joy, tears, fears, pressures, happiness, worry, fatigue, stress, to name but a few – a real melting pot. What I did really was quite simple. I just got out there and told my story and the reason I believed a Children's Hospice was vital from the most important perspective – the PARENTS. If there were no sick children (and how I wish there weren't), there would be no need for children's hospitals, or for this first children's hospice.

I found such amazing backing from those most important ordinary people, those with families who couldn't believe there wasn't already one. Parents whose children had their health were all so grateful for that, and wanted to help so much, hoping of course they would never need it. Those families who had sick children or had also lost children, knew even more so how necessary it was, and again, were spurred on to help, realising how wonderfully it could benefit their lives.

The people I found (and not all were of this ilk) not so pro-Children's Hospice were the medical fraternity. I guess I can understand why this is so, as they found it hard to deal with the fact that they could not make all children better. Therefore the need for palliative care, that is, LauraLynn House, was a bit of a taboo subject. The focus was (and to some degree, still is) constantly on home being the place to die, but the point being missed here is what a Children's Hospice is truly about – CHOICE.

Firstly, it is about making the best of the child's life (however short or long), especially where 24-hour care is required. As I always said, 'Putting life into a child's day, not days in a child's life'. It is about so much more though – fun, joy, living each minute, sharing the caring, giving breaks to the sick children. Vitally important, though, is giving the parents and other siblings the breaks in whatever way suits them best, and then, *choice* again, at the sad end, if home is not possible or the wish of the parents. With a few, it was hard to get that across, but most understood the difference it would make, and only wanted to help make it reality.

'Normal' everyday life is difficult enough, especially in ever more challenging times. Add to this the complex needs of a palliative care child, requiring 24-hour care, plus also caring for well siblings, and unless you live this reality you can only begin to *try* to imagine it.

The road has been full of twists, turns and strange coincidences, but it has been such a very interesting road to have walked. From large corporates, to ordinary people, like me, with everything imaginable in between, funds have come from far and wide. Whether big or small, it all added up to the donation which built, and is now running Ireland's first Children's Hospice.

I have worked very hard at answering every donor personally, as it is important to me that all know just how much their support means, and what a big part of LauraLynn House they truly are. I remember one of the first donations that came in was a Money Order for £5 (Irish pounds), and feeling bad that there was no way I could send my trademark thanks, as there was no accompanying letter. I hope if that person (and the subsequent few of the same since) reads this book, they will now know how much they mean. I always say, if it's only a cent, it's a cent we didn't have before we got it, and every cent truly does add up.

The years carried on, and Brendan and I were approached by a developer with a view to building LauraLynn House for us, as part of a development of residential property. He freely admitted he had his agenda, in that by doing this it would support him in his bid to have his land rezoned for housing. That was fine with us, of course, as it would bring our wonderful dream to fruition, and we would have our land and hospice even sooner than we might have dared to imagine.

That was our thinking at the time, and we went ahead, and even had plans drawn up as to how we wanted LauraLynn House to be developed. It was wonderful and exciting, but sadly that dream was shattered when the rezoning of the land was refused. That was the end of that opportunity and it just wasn't meant to be.

Eventually, through the support of the Irish Hospice Foundation, it was suggested that we meet up with staff from the Children's Sunshine Home in Foxrock, whose facility and criteria, at that time, was looking after intellectually disabled children. They were in the process of developing the facility, and branching into children's palliative care.

We went on to discuss the possibility of working together towards a merger. It made perfect sense, as the land and facility were already there, with medical, business and administration staff already in place. This of course would have to be developed and expanded on a greater scale, including the building of LauraLynn House, Ireland's first children's hospice.

I continued working away on my end, raising funds and awareness, and it took a few more years before we finalised the merger. Meanwhile, I joined the Board of Children's

Sunshine Home, and plans for building started. Many options and ideas were explored, including selling the land in Foxrock and moving to another larger site, but eventually it was decided to stay put, and on reflection the right decision was made. It is a beautiful and central location, accessible to many families easily enough.

The first sod was turned in September 2009, and it was an amazing day – a day so long awaited, particularly by Brendan and myself. The beginning of the reality of the original dream – what a milestone to have reached! Miriam O'Callaghan, who had become Patron of CSH/LauraLynn, was with us, and she did the honours beautifully as always.

The morning had started off quite dull, but at the right moment, the sun shone brightly – we definitely had some divine intervention! We had a lovely celebration, and again for Brendan and myself in particular it was a truly special time, shared with family and close friends. We celebrated, missed our girls even more than ever, but also felt them with us, and knew how happy they must be. Very poignant time, to put it mildly!

There was an interesting link with the building company ultimately chosen from those who tendered for the job of building LauraLynn House. The owner of the company, as it turned out, was my own late mother's godchild. It was a true twist of fate, and we both wondered what was going on in that place we call 'Heaven'? His parents were also gone, but we reminisced on the past a little, which was nice. We had grown up living close enough to one another, and I had also worked at different times in life with his two sisters. His wife, as it turned out, was a friend of a very close friend of mine as well. I felt again, as I often do, that divine powers of intervention were at work, as some things simply cannot always be put down to coincidence.

The next two years were long in some ways, but in other ways actually went by so quickly. The building went fairly smoothly, and was all pretty straightforward, with the builders very respectful of the children and staff there that they had to work around.

Another fantastic, if again very poignant day, was 27 September 2011 – the day LauraLynn House opened its doors. That particular Tuesday was the most amazing day in every way. The first thing was the weather – from early on, the sun shone so brightly and the heat was unreal, too hot really, but we were not complaining. I was a little nervous, as we had the wonderful honour of our beautiful and special President, Mary McAleese, coming to open the Hospice officially, and because of our special connection with her (see 'Lynn's Story' chapter), it was even more special for us. She was just at the end of her last term as President, so again timing was just right.

President McAleese spoke beautifully, as always, but of course said a lot of what I had in my head (I never speak using a script). I remember thinking to myself as I listened, 'what on earth am I going to say now?' I just had to go with what I had planned, and I guess I said much the same, but from my perspective, so in a different way to her. I think it all went fine but I was glad when it was over.

It was truly endearing to have our family, and many very close and dear friends, with us in the audience, and that was a special comfort for me. President McAleese got to speak with all the children and their families, and she was so natural and caring. Miriam O' Callaghan was also with us, and as always

Lynn and friends on her 9th birthday in 1995, the year we had Laura.

Siobhán and Lynn on holiday in Cork aged 7 (left) and aged 11 (right),
in Levi's pub/shop in Ballydehob (see Phil Cherry story, page 139)

Siobhán, Lynn, Laura on Graduation day from NDNSP, 1998.

Lynn and her Aunty (and Godmother) Irene, on holiday in Spain in 1997.

Siobhán and Lynn going to Fancy Dress party, a Patsy and Edwina from Ab Fab.

Gillian shaving Lynn's head in 1999
– Lynn smiled, as I tried not to cry.

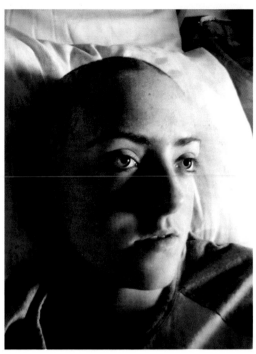

Beautiful photo of Lynn, taken by one of
the consultants in Our Lady's.

Sitting watching TV after head shave – how brave and beautiful she was!

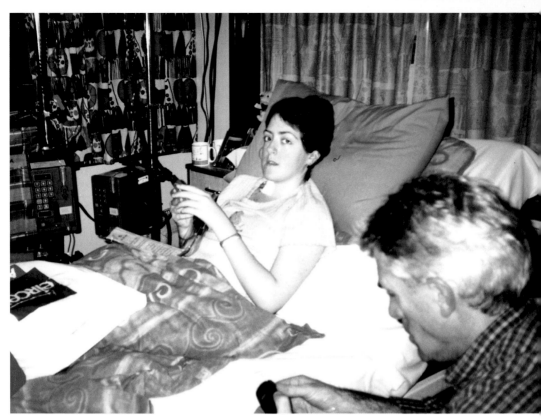

Lynn (14) back in Our Lady's after relapse, and before she lost her hair, once more.

Lynn modelling at a Fashion Show, organised by my friends and work colleagues in the Courts Service, to raise funds for a holiday for us. It was a fantastic evening in the Gresham Hote

Lynn modelling a more favoured outfit.

Lynn and Siobhán having fun dressing up and modelling that evening.

Driving the Porsche Carrera 911, which her friend Ciara's Dad brought along in those last weeks. Jimmy took the girls and his son for a drive, and apparently Lynn wanted him to go faster and faster. I laughed, as she obviously thought, 'What the heck, I'm dying anyway!

Me, Dolores, Brendan, Siobhán, Lynn and Gillian in Bunratty, an evening out as part of her Make-Wish treat. Lady Emma putting on our bibs (she later found fame with the group 'Six', and as a T presenter). What a fun evening we all had.

Siobhán's 15th birthday – December 2000. Lynn had relapsed, but it didn't stop her having fun.

Siobhán, me and Lynn in Cruzzos restaurant in Malahide. Phil, Siobhán and family hired a limo and treated us to a most wonderful day out – one of our special memories, even though our daughter was dying.

Lynn and Nicky Byrne. In Dublin airport, on our way to Dromoland Castle for Lynn's Make-a-Wish, Lynn met Westlife, who were flying on their private plane to Manchester for their concert. Lynn had them all to herself, and they took photos and signed autographs. We didn't know then that she would see them again and have a special time with them a few days later.

Siobhán and Lynn at dinner in Dromoland Castle. I often look at this photo and wonder again at her courage, but also wonder, 'what were you really thinking, my sweet darling?'

Bunratty again, and the girls having fun. Lynn, Sibhy and Gill with one of the Pipers.

worked her job as Patron and MC in the most caring way. The President then unveiled the lovely plaque, spoke for another little while to the children and families, and then headed off to her next appointment.

I had so many friends come and chat and have photos taken, it was hard to keep up, but also so special, and I know everyone was delighted that at last we had our Children's Hospice. No doubt, no one was happier than the parents and sick children who would spend time there – precious time making special memories, with their sick little darlings. The day continued with lovely celebrations and Brendan and I were presented with a beautiful painting of LauraLynn House, which hangs proudly in our dining area and which we will always treasure.

I will always remember that very lovely day, possibly the greatest and most special of my memories through this long journey. I do, however, take away other special memories of events and occasions – things (as Lynn said in her last weeks) that in another life I would never have experienced. There was a beautiful program called *Would You Believe* made on our story some years back, and while it was so very emotional, it was also a lovely memory to our girls. It very much helped the charity too, and was a truly special time, spent with those involved – all part of Lynn's and Laura's lives.

I was also interviewed on the *Gerry Kelly Show* in Belfast, which I think gave me the courage to do further media in the future. I was subsequently asked to do the *Late Late Show*, when Pat Kenny was still hosting, and although I thought I would never be able for it, I was actually very relaxed. Again, it brought so much awareness and support to LauraLynn, it was unreal. The letters I got from people who said it helped them in their situations meant so much to me, as that is more what it's about than anything. If any of us can help one person out there, in even the smallest way, it is a wonderful thing. It certainly gives more to the 'giver' than the 'receiver'.

Since then, I have done many TV and radio interviews, and all have been great in bringing support and a higher profile to the charity, which is so important to me.

I was also honoured to be nominated for, and chosen to receive, a 'People of the Year' award in 2007. I was so touched just to have been nominated. I accepted the award on behalf of all who had and were supporting LauraLynn. This event also led to more wonderful support and funding.

I had another lovely and very unexpected honour bestowed some years later by the American Ireland Fund, who invited me to be the 'Honoree' at their Gala Dinner in Boston in 2010. The Fund treated Brendan and I royally and made our stay in Boston very memorable. They have been wonderful supporters of LauraLynn House, and as with all our supporters we remain truly grateful to them.

There have been other awards/events throughout the years, and while these occasions are not really 'my thing' or what I'm about (and there are far more deserving people) I have appreciated them all and extend my sincere thanks to everyone involved.

September 2015 – LauraLynn House today

It is hard to believe we are now heading into our fifth year since LauraLynn House opened. Over that time we have brought special care and comfort to many precious sick little ones, and to their families. A TV Documentary called *No Time to Die* was made about three very brave families who lived at and received home care from LauraLynn. I have been so lucky to have had the wonderful privilege of knowing two of those families and meeting their beautiful children (they tell their stories in this book). I am also so happy as they have told me time and time again how LauraLynn gave their angels a life, as full as it could possibly be, how it gave them a life as a family, and most importantly, how it left them with very precious memories. They would never have had these if they had to struggle alone or with limited support.

There are many wonderful new programmes being developed at LauraLynn House, such as sibling camps, parent pampering days, music therapy, play therapy, educational programmes and much more. Thanks to funding raised by Ray D'Arcy's Half Millon Half Marathon, LauraLynn@Home Project, launched by Miriam O' Callaghan in June 2014, is an additional wonderful support now in place. Exciting times, and it is so special to be able to do what we do – help our treasured families.

7

Jane's Diaries

'All of me loves all of you, even your
perfect imperfections.'

Since Laura died on 31 August 1999, I have written diaries to her, and subsequently to Lynn, and some cross over letters to both, on certain occasions.

In the first year after Laura's death, I wrote every day to Laura. I think it was both a form of comfort and a healing of sorts. At least that's the only way I can explain it to you.

I wrote as if I was talking to my little angel, and on most pages, I asked, sometimes begged, her to mind and help our 'Linnie'. I'm sure she did her best to help Lynn, and I know from one of the little diaries Lynn did leave behind that she too prayed to Laura, and had some comfort in that. She did say, though, that she wondered sometimes if Laura was listening, could hear her, or even if there was anyone or anything there at all? I have to say, I concur with those sentiments often, but like Lynn, have to now believe both my girls are there somewhere, and here by my side often, giving me strength, comfort and courage. I do hope so. I know they are definitely together and at peace.

After Lynn died, I wrote to both my angels on their birthdays, anniversaries, Christmas, Easter, which always falls around Lynn's anniversary, and on special occasions like 'People of Year' awards, turning of the sod and opening of LauraLynn, to name but a few. I actually think my girls must find some of the things that have happened to me hilarious. I can almost hear them say, 'Look at our crazy Mam – what on earth is she going to do next?' Most of all, though, I hope they are proud, and certainly know they will be happy that we continue not just to exist, but actually live a life. They will, without doubt, also be very happy that something so good, to help others, was born from our loss of them.

My diaries are several books long now, as Laura is gone 16 years and Lynn 14, but I never tire of writing, as I find it a source of comfort, and keeps my girls close to me – almost like they are still here. The following are a few entries I've chosen to share.

Chats to Laura – one year after my sweet angel has died

31ˢᵗ August 2000 - Laura's first anniversary.

My darling beautiful Laura,

I'm a little late writing this, but I know you won't mind. Today was a busy and sad day for us all. So many people thought of you and missed you, but no one more so than me. I love you so much and miss you so desperately. You were the light that brightened my days for all of your short, sweet little life. I never thought this time last year that you would leave me, but Holy God needed you, and didn't want or need you to suffer this life any longer. Sometimes lately, I think you are much better off, not suffering the pain of this world, but that doesn't stop my heart aching, and my arms longing to hold you tight and kiss and love you. I hope you don't miss me as much as I miss you, because the pain is so hard to bear. I'll try to be happy for you angel, but it's just not easy, so forgive me if I don't succeed. I hope you enjoyed Lynn and Siobhan talking about you this evening, and I'm glad Lynn cried, as she misses you so desperately - you are the beautiful sister she waited so long to have and love. Look after her, little sweet, and watch over her always. Thanks for giving me strength to go on. Come to me again when you can - I loved that great big hug the other night in my dreams. Tell Lorraine we love and miss her too. Have fun and be happy and some day I'll be happy with you again - we all will. Look after your Daddy, Linnie and me - we love and miss you forever - until we meet again.

All our love, and all the hugs and kisses I can give you, my angel,

Mammy xxxx

Last entry I wrote to Laura, before Lynn died

19th February 2001

Hello, Beautiful Angel,

It's a while since I wrote to you, and a lot has happened since then, as you must surely know. Poor 'Linnie' had such a terrible time, with the fitting. It was all so frightening for her and for us. Sweet darling - I love her so much, and don't want to see her suffer. Please ask Holy God to help her get better, but not to suffer any more - she's been through enough, and never complains. Please help us all to get through the next few months, get through the bone marrow transplant, and come out okay on the other side. Little sweetheart, you are happy now - no pain, no worries any longer!! I'm so sure you are in a beautiful peaceful place, and I hope I am right in my thinking. I miss you more and more each passing day, and my heart constantly aches for you. You're a part of me that's gone forever, until we meet again. I love you so, my sweet Laura,

Mammy xxxx

Next entry to my two girls, as Lynn has gone now to join her little sister in paradise

21 July 2001

Hello to my two sweet and beautiful girls - together once again, and happy now forever,

Little did I know on the 19th February, when I last wrote, that next time I did, you too would have left us and this earth also Lynn. I had such hope then that you would somehow get through, and get better. I know how much you wanted to and how hard you tried. But it wasn't to be. You were so very brave and strong beyond belief, my sweet darling. You accepted all your pain and suffering, both physical and mental, with such courage and dignity. Thank you so much for all the love and help you have given to me. You already know that I miss you and Laura so desperately and my pain is unbearable beyond words. I am comforted a little though, when I think of you both together now, and I envy you having each other, when I am so lonely without you. Is Laura still so cute and beautiful, as you wondered and talked to me about in your last week of life Lynn? I'm sure you know I've watched the videos of you both lately, and though I cried bitterly, also found such comfort in them. Sadness too, of course that you are gone from this world and your Daddy and me. How is Lorraine? No doubt, you are all having fun hanging out together. I long for the day when I can be with you again, but I will try for your sakes to make the best of the life and health, i know I'm so lucky to have. How long that life will be for, I don't know!! I know this is what you would wish, but you will need to help me along the way, as much as you can. Thanks for the 'watch' episode Lynn - gave me so much comfort, and I knew you would give me a sign, if you could, and I hope more to come.

Well, my angels, I'll finish now, but I'll write again soon. I love you both always and forever, and am so glad that I had you for as long as I did. I just wish it could have been forever, and you had to bury me, instead of the other way round. You brought me so much joy and happiness, and I'll always be grateful for the beautiful and magic years together. I do know that you'll be by my side always, and that you'll mind me and Daddy, who's also so totally broken hearted.

My love, hugs and kissed Laura & Linnie,

Mammy xxxxxxxxxxxxxxxxxxxxx

First Christmas since both our girls have gone

25ᵗʰ December 2002

Lynn & Laura,

My wonderful girls - you know how much I miss you on this Christmas Eve/Day. More than words can say, and more than ever, each passing moment. You fill my thoughts from morning 'till night, and even my in my sleeping hours. I can hardly believe another year has passed - no Santa, no excited shopping for presents, no happiness, just emptiness. Only bit of comfort is that I feel you both close to me always, though you are no longer here. I just wish I could see you both, just one more time. Hear you, touch you, talk to you, laugh with you, see your beautiful smiles. I can only imagine it now, and that's just not the same. It's like dying with thirst, seeing some water, but not being able to reach it. I am so lonely, it is almost unbearable. I know I have your Dad, who is also so sad, lonely and broken. I have many people here for me, but

I don't want any of them - I just want you, my precious babies back.

I hope though, my angels, that you are having an exciting Christmas wherever you are, minding each other now, and I hope that Santa has come to you there. Give my love to Lorraine too, and you 3 musketeers must look after us all here, and give us courage and strength to carry on, in this very sad world of ours. Miss you and love you with all my heart for ever and ever - my sweet Laura & Lynn,

Mammy xxxxx

Start of another year

1ˢᵗ January 2003

Hello, my sweet darlings,

The only thing positive about the start of another year is that I am a year closer to seeing you both again, and then we will be together for ever. I don't know what's wrong with me lately, but I seem to hate everything and everyone - maybe hate is the wrong word - maybe it's just lack of tolerance with life? I suppose if I'm honest, it's anger at what is mostly my huge sadness at my loss of my beautiful girls, and I feel bad about that, as anger is not in my nature really. Forgive me, my feelings please. I know you will not like me this way, and I'm sure it will pass with time.

I can't even begin to imagine the years ahead being any different, except that if I'm going to survive in this world, I guess I'll have to push myself with what I hope will be a saving grace for me, a tribute to you Lynn & Laura, and a happiness of a kind for children like you two, and their families. Please send me in the right direction and help me along the way. I wish I could feel the genuine strength I know I need to carry on - maybe by some miracle, it will come.

I hope, pray, and have to believe you are both so happy together in a wonderful place and I'm so sorry to be a blight on that happiness. I have to try harder. I love you both so, so much and miss forever what might have been. Feel my arms around you and I'll try to feel yours around me,

My eternal love,

Mammy xxxx

My most recent entry – Laura's 16th anniversary

Dear Laura,

Sixteen years since you left this world and our hearts broke in two. Lynn's heart shattered also, and then, what she had to face herself. The end of life for you sweet angel, and sadly, the beginning of the end for lovely Linnie. Your anniversary is always the saddest, my sweet, as it always brings up the enormity of the horror of that fateful evening on the 30th. Then, what Lynn had to face herself, before going to be with you forever. I miss you so much little sweet, and wonder each passing year, how you would look and what you'd be doing in life.

I see others around yours and Lynn's ages, and how life is for them and with them, the milestone birthdays, weddings, babies, etc. and while I'm so very happy for them, I can't help but question why you had to go? Of course, as I've said many times, no answers to that question!

I hope you and Linnie are happy and at peace, holding each other's hands, as I know you hold mine. It's so good that I do feel you both with me, minding me always, and guiding me along my road. In the 'departure lounge' now but I hope I do you both proud as I try to 'LIVE' the life you surely wish me to.

Thank you for the joyous years you gave me darling and Linnie too. I know I am so lucky to have had that - the most wonderful gift in the world - one's children and the love they bring, as you both did for me.

Eternal love & big hugs,

Mammy

8

Special Friends and Supporters of
LauraLynn House

'Friends are like snowflakes that never melt.'

Jill Barrett:

Tale of an errant tractor driver

In my teens I saw a television documentary on Helen House, the UK's and the world's first children's hospice. Having only ever been to the funerals of elderly people, it seemed inconceivable to me that children should die. Much later in life I saw Jane for the first time, on *The Late Late Show*. Like so many, I was struck by her story but also by the realisation that, almost 20 years after the UK had built its first, and subsequently many other hospices for children we didn't have even one. 'It's about putting life into a child's day,' Jane said, 'not days into a child's life.' Those words sat in my mind for weeks. I wrote them into my address book with Jane's number.

A few years later my work colleagues and I did the minimarathon for LauraLynn and I had the honour of meeting Jane for the first time. I was late as usual (sorry Jane) but she was the lady she always is and greeted me with the same warm smile that she radiates to all she meets. You can't but get a sense of the spirit of Laura and Lynn when you meet Jane and Brendan; they are so much a part of their presence.

In 2007 I took a career break from work with the view of stepping out of the rat race and taking some time to chill out. By the second week I was already bored and wondered what useful project might occupy my time. It took only seconds for LauraLynn to spring to mind. Having completed (at a pace any self-respecting snail would be embarrassed by) more 10k runs than you could shake a stick at, I decided on a tractor drive, as a testament to my amazing Dad, George Barrett. My equally insane cousin Louise volunteered to share the driving and 'TractorOnTour' was born.

A couple of weeks later I found myself wandering around the National Ploughing Championships begging for the loan of a tractor. I met Ray Quinn and his team at New Holland and the rest is history. On 18 April 2008 (Lynn's 7th anniversary) we departed Kelly's Ford Dealers in Kilcock (where my Dad used to sell Ford tractors, the predecessors to New Hollands) on Ireland's first, and still *only*, all-female-driven 32-county tractor drive. Our mode of transport was a shiny new T7030. For those of you that don't (yet) know your tractors, New Hollands are the deep blue ones with the yellow logo. Any light blue, green or red tractors are suspect.

It was a journey we'll never forget – not just the immediate team of me, Louise, her friends and mine – but also multiple family members, journalists, photographers, sponsors, web support people, gardaí and police to name a few, and all those people in all corners of Ireland who had never heard of LauraLynn – those who laughed with us, cried with us, told us their own stories and donated €115,000 to a cause that no-one can ignore.

I think that Laura and Lynn might have laughed at something that happened on the final day when we arrived back into Kilcock. As we pulled the tractor up I asked their Dad, affectionately referred to by me as AF, or 'the Aul' Fella', to join me in the tractor for a drive around Kilcock village. I should say here that I've since changed AF to YF, 'the Young Fella', both for reasons of needing to survive and, well, because Bren and Jane are both candidates for the lead roles in *The Curious Case of Benjamin Button and His Wife*. At first he was reluctant (he had obviously seen my tractor driving) but finally agreed and hopped into the passenger seat. As I navigated my way at speed through Kilcock's one-way, very narrow streets, with cars and their vulnerable wing mirrors on all sides, I could see his grip tightening on the side of the tractor and the blood draining from his face. His sense of relief at getting back on to solid ground as our 'spin' ended was palpable, so thanks YF for 'feeling the fear and doing it anyway'.

People often asked what the best part of the trip was and one of the most special was being invited on a walk-around Horizon House, Northern Ireland's first children's hospice. Despite the terrible circumstances that necessitate its being, it is a place of love, calm and laughter, a place where children can be children. As I was leaving I thought how amazing it would be when one day, thanks to the most special family that is the McKennas, I would visit the Republic's first children's hospice, and so it came to be.

I don't know when my day to leave this life will come. I know that for Jane and Brendan, Laura and Lynn's day came too soon. Because of them I got to do something that I would never otherwise have done. Because of them I got to meet people I'd never have met. Because of them I got to see parts of Ireland I'd still never have seen. Because of them I got to experience the most unbelievable display of human warmth, kindness and generosity that will last me a lifetime. And for all those things and so much more I will be forever grateful for Laura, Lynn, Jane and Brendan – thank you.

Maureen Fitzpatrick:

My journey with the LauraLynn began back in November 2000. My daughter Emma had just been diagnosed with a rare form of Non-Hodgkin's Lymphoma. We were devastated and scared. We had been sent straight to Crumlin to begin treatment. I met Jane McKenna in the kitchen of St. John's ward in Crumlin, and as we exchanged stories I was horrified to hear the ordeal Jane was going through. Her daughter Lynn's cancer had just relapsed after a short time in remission. This alone would be any parent's worst nightmare, but Jane and Brendan were dealing with this on top of the grief of losing their only other daughter Laura a short time earlier. I can still see Jane pacing up and down the corridors with Lynn. Lynn was a beautiful, tall girl. I didn't really get to know Jane until a few years later but thought of her often. When we returned to Crumlin a few weeks later, I wondered where Jane was. I knew she was due to return with Lynn around that time for treatment. However, I was told that Lynn had since passed away. I wondered how life could be so cruel, and how Jane would ever find the strength to cope. This was my first encounter with death in Crumlin and I thought of Jane and Brendan often. Strangely, I got comfort in knowing that if they had the strength to cope, maybe we would too.

Unfortunately, as the days, weeks and months passed we slowly came to the realisation that Emma wasn't going to get any better. She was getting weaker all the time and none of the chemotherapy or radiation seemed to be working. On Wednesday the 11th of July, our worst fears were confirmed. The doctors and all the staff in Crumlin were amazing, but there was nothing more they could do for Emma. She was being sent home to die. Although, in the back of our minds we knew things weren't good, nothing prepares you for being told that news. We were numb and heartbroken. Emma returned home. Thanks to the kindness of Bishop Leo O'Reilly, she received her Confirmation at home on the 14th of July, surrounded by family and friends. I remember being at a Mass in Crumlin for bereaved parents before I left, and the priest admitted he couldn't explain why God would make children suffer and take them so young. But one thing he did reassure us of was that God would send someone in our path that will help us along the way. Jane was one of those people for me. The other person for us was Father Dan, our parish priest at the time, and now a dear family friend. He was amazing. A day wouldn't pass without him coming to pray with us, bless us, to reassure us and support us. He wrote the most beautiful funeral homily for Emma.

Emma was such an outgoing, brave and kind little girl. She was the second youngest of six children. She was always wise beyond her years and had a great sense of humour. She never complained, and even in her final weeks wanted to enjoy life. Even with the need of a wheelchair most of the time because she was too weak to walk, Emma still attended any event she could in the local festival. Her beloved dog 'Tibby' won a prize in the dog show, and she won the Children's Fancy Dress. She even attended the 'Beat on the Street' and the treasure hunt. Emma appreciated every minute she was on this earth, and taught us all a lot about how we should live our lives. Emma was selfless. One of the last messages Fr. Dan received from Emma was on the 15th August 2001, at 00:31, and it reads *'That would be lovely father. Thank you. Say a prayer for Michelle please. Emma'.* She was thanking Fr. Dan for his offer to bring her Holy Communion the next morning and asking him to pray for her sister Michelle who was due to get her Leaving Cert results the next day. She was always thinking of others, even in her final days. She was especially close to her younger sister, Laura, and was very protective of her. Emma was such a special little girl and it broke our hearts to lose her. Sadly, there was to be no miracle for Emma, but I often think that we were blessed with a miracle, and that was the ability to cope.

We were very blessed in that we were able to care for Emma at home in her final days, as we had huge support from family and friends. Some families aren't so lucky and need a place like the LauraLynn House to provide palliative care to terminally ill children. Even during a time of unimaginable grief, Jane and Brendan McKenna recognised the huge need for a children's hospice in Ireland, and in 2002 began the long and arduous process of fundraising to create a Hospice dedicated to the memory of their two beautiful daughters.

I first began fundraising for the LauraLynn in 2004. My friend Geraldine encouraged me to make a call to Jane to see how we could help fundraise. That year we hoped to raise €1,000 for the Hospice, but with huge efforts and support from family and friends, went on to raise €22,000. In the coming years, we completed mini marathons, car boot sales and other activities and raised over €120,000 for LauraLynn House. We were all inspired by Jane, and were amazed how she could be so selfless and find the strength to do what she was doing.

Shortly before it opened in 2011, Jane invited us to visit LauraLynn House. LauraLynn House truly is an amazing place, full of warmth and caring comfort for many families living with very sick children. It's also a reminder of how fragile life can be, and how we need to be so thankful for the blessings we have in life, and not take anything for granted. Jane and Brendan McKenna are two of the strongest and most selfless people you could ever hope to meet. They are an inspiration, and have showed us all that even in times of the most unimaginable tragedy, amazing things can be done. LauraLynn House is a symbol of hope and is a fantastic tribute to Laura and Lynn. We are very proud to be a part of it.

I would like to thank Jane and Brendan McKenna for their kind invitation to write a piece for their book. I would also like to thank all those who were so kind and supportive in fundraising for LauraLynn House over the years.

Dedicated to the memory of our beloved daughter, sister, aunt and friend, Emma Fitzpatrick (1989-2001)

Dr. Dolores King:

Jane and I met as teens working in the Civil Service in 1974.
We quickly became firm friends and our lives have been
intertwined ever since, as were our future husbands, children
and extended families. We were together through the highs
and lows of young adulthood; Jane losing her mother to cancer
at 20 years old; me marrying Liam at 20 years old and having
two daughters, Lorraine and Gillian, two and a bit years later.
Jane married Brendan shortly after and had Lynn a few years
later. A few years after that I had a son, Sean. In 1994 we both
were pregnant together for the first time. I had another son,
Daire, and Jane had Laura four months later. Even though we
were not blood relations, the children considered themselves
to be cousins. We journeyed through life's milestones together.
For two decades, until the mid-1990s, our lives were pretty
normal. We experienced the joys and struggles of life. Then
our lives changed forever. We all experienced the saddest,
most challenging decade of our lives, which each of us has
been coming to terms with ever since.

The joy of Laura's birth was very quickly followed by her
diagnosis. Her short, precious life was a struggle with illness.
She also brought such joy to everybody around her. It was
like she made the best of every minute, exuding love and
excitement. While Laura was awaiting the surgery to 'make
her better', our beautiful Lorraine, who was now almost 21
years old, was diagnosed with Leukaemia. Our lives crashed
down around us. Lorraine was beautiful inside and out,
a shining light. She touched all of us deeply and still does.
Laura lost her battle with life and Lorraine lost hers 10 weeks
later, on her 22nd birthday. Laura was four and a half years

old. Lynn's diagnosis, the day before Laura died, and while Lorraine was struggling through the last weeks of her life, was almost unbearable. We remained optimistic for Lynn, thinking, 'lightning cannot strike for a third time'. Life could not be that cruel. We had high hopes that Lynn would make it through her illness but it was not to be. She showed such dignity, maturity and strength as she braved her illness and had no doubt that her 'two angels' were waiting for her as she approached death. She was 15 years and 1 month old.

I have learned a lot about life and death, strength and resilience. I have learned how to live life to the fullest and have lost the fear of death. I have learned these lessons from the three girls, witnessing their strength and dignity as they journeyed through life, accepting their fate, to the end. I have learned from the life and death of others close to me. Although the loss is unbearable, it was a privilege to witness these things. I have also learned from my three children who were left behind to deal with such enormous grief at such young ages. We could not understand it as grown adults, I don't know how they managed to cope at all. However, they have developed into mature, caring adults, knowing how to support others at difficult times. We have all found ways to move forward with our lives, at times with great difficulty. I guess we have all gained strength from our experiences. We wouldn't have chosen the experiences, yet we were privileged to be part of the life and death and legacy left behind by our daughters' and sisters' short lives. We will carry them in our hearts forever. Nothing will ever fill the space that the loss left in our hearts. I guess a little bit of us goes with each person we lose.

However, life does go on and we gain strength from our experiences. Perhaps the main message from our story is that the human spirit is so resilient and that so many positive things can come from such heartbreak. The LauraLynn Children's Hospice is a testament to that.

Cathy McCarthy:

My journey with Jane – Strangers who became friends

> *'Some people come into our lives, leave footprints in our hearts and minds and we are never the same again.'* Flavia Weedn

My friendship with Jane has an unusual beginning. In February of 2002 I was driving down Newtownpark Avenue, heading for Blackrock, when I was listening to *The Pat Kenny Show*. It was a beautiful morning and I had not a care in the world. Pat read a letter from Jane McKenna. It told a story of losing her two children. The letter linked her tragic loss with the 9/11 bombings. The main point of her letter and what she was trying to convey was her gratitude at being able to say goodbye to her two beautiful girls, Laura and Lynn. She was talking about the 9/11 tragedy and as bad as her situation was, her whole point was that she had time to say goodbye to her children. At this time my youngest son Jack was preparing for his first communion. I was at a loss for words and I had an enormous sense of gratitude for my own life and the people in it. I was so touched by the letter that I wrote to Jane. Jane replied to me with a lovely card. As I now know, but did not then, Jane hand-writes a personal card to everyone who contacts her. It is a touch that is unique to Jane. I put the card away and thought nothing more of it. About a year later I was searching for a voucher my husband gave to me as a birthday present and which I could not locate. I decided to empty my bedside locker and in the midst of the search I found Jane's card. For some reason on reading the card again I made a decision to write to her to see how she was getting on. Jane again replied and suggested that we might talk on the phone. We did that and a beautiful friendship began. We came together as strangers and are now the best of friends. Oh, and by the way, I also found the voucher.

In around 2005 I had a coffee morning in my home for LauraLynn. It was a wonderful morning and anyone who met Jane was instantly struck by her inspiration and presence. Since then I have taken an active part in LauraLynn and I frequently accompany Jane to fundraising events. I joke with Jane that I am her Southside representative. The fundraising over many years resulted in the opening of LauraLynn House in September 2011. I know from talking to people that I have met that LauraLynn House is a place where they can get support for their very ill children. Her vision to set up LauraLynn House has brought light and hope to so many parents.

I have to mention Brendan, Jane's husband. Brendan is the quiet presence in the background. He is a great support to Jane with his advice and encouragement when it is needed. It is a privilege to know Jane and Brendan. I am blessed that Jane and I have crossed paths on life's journey. Her footprint and legacy will remain long after she is gone.

'There is no perfect path, only a perfectly authentic
You – full of contradictions, uniqueness and gifts. It

is your You-ness that allows you truly to light up the world with your presence. Your You-ness is lifetimes in the making. It is your flaws, your quirks, your weirdness, your ancestral history, your gifts, your humour, and your imperfections. Your light and message will come through you regardless of what path you choose. Your authentic self emerges when you follow what lights you up, or in other words, when you do what you love. And then do it in a way that only you can. Our soul is always calling us towards what will light us up.' Rebecca Campbell

Michele McNaughton:

My friendship with Jane Mc Kenna started 10 years ago over a cup of coffee in Bewleys on Grafton Street. At the time I was Showroom Manager for a tile company and the employees had raised money for the LauraLynn Foundation. Jane had agreed to meet me so I could give her the cheque. The minute we met we just clicked and a true, true friendship was born, not only with her but her husband Brendan, who is also an amazing person. It was on that day I decided that I wanted to get involved personally and help Jane any way I could.

Over the years I have watched Jane in awe as she continually works very hard to raise money for LauraLynn House, and to make people aware how very important it is to have a Children's Hospice and respite for very sick children and their families. The amount of time that Jane has spent trying to raise the money for this wonderful cause would put everyone to shame. I love spending time with Jane – she is such a caring and loving person who you can just be yourself with.

I personally feel privileged that Jane and Brendan invited me to be involved in the building of LauraLynn House. It was an exciting time and one got an overwhelming feeling to see Jane and Brendan's dream come true. For what should be a very sad place it is quite the opposite. You walk in and all you see is happiness and laughter. It's a lovely, bright 'home away from home', and you just feel you belong and are taken care of.

No one ever thinks they will lose a child, but to lose two children must have brought both great sorrow and heartbreak. Some people would not be able to recover from such a loss, but this is where I believe they got their strength which made them stronger. Their beautiful daughters will never be forgotten, as their memory will always live on. Jane and Brendan, you should be so proud and I'm so lucky I can call you my friends.

Pauline Melia:

I first met Jane McKenna when we were both working in the legal profession. We immediately had something in common. My daughter Amanda was very sick in hospital and while talking, Jane told me about her little Laura, who was awaiting heart surgery. Sadly, everyone knows Laura did not survive the surgery and Lynn got leukaemia. The Courts Service organised a Fashion Show while Lynn was in remission to raise funds for Leukaemia research. Lynn was asked to model on the show and I can still see Jane Brendan and Lynn, walking into the crazy dressing room beforehand. I remember thinking how overwhelmed they looked and what they were going through was a nightmare. They were wonderful and Lynn shone on the catwalk and was allowed to keep the clothes she modelled. The total shock and devastation hit so many when Lynn passed away.

Jane and I became good friends and she had started on the road of the hospice despite all odds. I am so proud to say I have accompanied Jane on many occasions on that road and the day of the opening was just a dream come through. I, in all those years, have never heard Jane ask anyone for funds, but have heard her thanking people for their contributions. These events, whether very large functions or small Town Halls and Community Centres, whether the amount was large or small, it never made any difference. Jane would appreciate every euro contributed. That's Jane and that's how people have been so drawn to this charity.

I can say truly, I have recommended some families to this wonderful 'home from home' and the difference it has made to their lives is unbelievable. All this because of one woman's determination to help other familes.

Brendan, has always stayed in the background, but has been there every step of the way on this journey. His support for Jane and the Hospice, whilst dealing with the loss of his beautiful daughters, could not have been easy. Brendan is a wonderful Dad, husband and a really good friend.

Amanda Melia:

I grew up with the name of LauraLynn in my home. My Mam had become friends with Jane and Brendan and very involved with the charity.

I was only six years old when I modelled on a Fashion Show with Lynn in the Gresham Hotel and always remember the excitement and fun we all had.

Laura had already passed away but I did meet Lynn and she was beautiful.

I accompanied Jane and my Mam to so many events, where funds were being raised and hence I grew up with the LauraLynn being a big part of my life. I am so proud of that and having seen the former President of Ireland, Mary McAleese, officially opening the house, children in the house with their parents, at the Christmas Fair and Memorial Services – it leaves lasting memories in my heart.

After Lynn passed away, while visiting Jane and Brendan at home, I always remember the effort Brendan made to play with me, and in fact the two of us got into trouble as we were playing ball in the front room. Looking back on that day and many others, it must have been so hard having a child in the house again. They are fantastic people and I am so glad my Mam became friends all those years ago as we consider them family now.

Ciara Murray:

Jane and I have been friends for thirty years – three decades and a mountain of memories. We met, as I made the giant leap from school to the workplace, Jane opened the door to let me in on my first day and her smile and welcome was what I needed, to settle my nerves. Jane already knew my Dad because he worked as a part-time handy man – Jack of all trades, master of none, Jane will know what I mean – for my new employer. We both had no idea what life had in store for us, how serious illness and heart-breaking loss would affect us in different ways and shape our worlds forever. We have remained solid friends since that morning, and there have been many times that Jane has been my shoulder to cry on and the push that I needed to keep going. I hope, in some small way, that I have managed to do the same for Jane and Brendan. Jane and I now meet as often as our busy lives allow us to, our dates usually involve food, on a good day a glass or two of wine! We always manage to make time for a little retail therapy, a visit to TK Maxx for my fix – Lynn would approve as Jane would testify she had all the makings of a serious follower of fashion. We laugh, sometimes cry, debate/discuss the ifs, whys and buts of our lives, and always talk about the girls. We pack a lot into our time together – something that we have learned from Lynn.

I am what people refer to as one of the lucky ones. I have survived cancer myself and I was in the early stages of remission when Lynn was diagnosed. Because I had battled the disease, it was very hard for me to watch Lynn so young take on this monster. She faced it like a true warrior, was well able to ask questions and wanted to know what was happening. She approached her illness with maturity way beyond her short years. She did know something about the condition because of Lorraine, Dolores' daughter, who had lost her own battle to cancer. Lynn did struggle with many things but she did not complain – that would have been a waste of time – instead she channelled her energies into getting through her treatment so that she could make it home, even if it was only for a couple of hours.

Home was where Lynn's heart was and every minute spent there was so precious. My mam Beth would go in to see her armed with prayers, relics and bottles of holy water from the four corners of Ireland. My mam always had somewhere to be and time keeping was never her strong point. She would in mid-sentence realise that she needed to be somewhere else and take off in a gallop that would give any race horse a run for their money, leaving Jane, Brendan and Lynn in hysterics. Brendan still talks and laughs about my mam's speedy exits from the ward to this day. My mam's health is rapidly deteriorating and she suffers from acute memory loss. She carries a key ring of the girls on her main set of keys and she firmly believes that they keep her safe. When she loses these keys, which happens on a regular basis, she calls on her two angels to come to her rescue – so thanks girls.

When Lynn's treatment failed and there was no hope, Jane and Brendan took her home. Their hearts were already broken into a million pieces, but they gave their all to making the short time that Lynn had left fun, happy and memorable – her phone call with Ronan Keating springs to mind. She was surrounded by her family and friends in the place that she felt safe and secure, where she had lived, loved and laughed (so much) with her little sister Laura and her Mam and Dad. At fifteen, Lynn bravely put her affairs in order, shared a few selective secrets and made her instructions known. She categorized the things she wanted to have with her as she made her final journey to be reunited with Laura and Lorraine. For all of us left behind, it brought some comfort knowing that she was on her way to the girls. Lynn wanted her Mam and Dad to carry on and in my opinion they have done an incredible job so far.

Lynn died at home and this was what she wanted. Jane and Brendan nursed Lynn themselves, they did have some support but it was limited because there was very little palliative care for children available at this time. Like so many others, I am so proud of the work that Jane and Brendan have done and continue to do tirelessly, in memory of the girls, to make the changes that were needed to provide hospice care for children with life limiting diseases. My sister and I visited LauraLynn House before it officially opened and it is a truly special place. For all those parents who walk through the doors with their sick children there are no happy endings but there are lots of happy times.

Laura came to my wedding in August 1994 in Jane's tummy and she was very well behaved! It was a shock and sad to hear that Laura was born with a heart defect. She was a second Shirely Temple with a fabulous head of sausage ringlets! Laura had a very distinctive breathing sound because of her heart defect, and at times would have a bluish complexion, but it just added to her charm.

Despite her health issue, Laura was a happy little girl and packed so much into her short life. She adored her big sister Lynn. For me, she was a mini-Jane from a personality point of view and Lynn was more like her Dad.

Jane dressed Laura in one of my niece Emma's dresses for her journey to heaven, and I have always felt that a little part of Emma went with her to keep her safe. Jane, being Jane, hoped my sister would not mind. I think this is a testimony to Jane's nature that even though she was about to bury her beautiful baby there was still room for consideration for others.

Jane was honoured with a 'People of the Year' award and I was very privileged to be with her on the night when she received her truly deserved accolade. Of course, Jane and I had gone on an extensive shopping trip for our outfits and did serious credit card damage beforehand. My husband, sister and brother-in-law came and it was a rare opportunity for us all to put on our glad rags and rub shoulders with the elite of the Irish celebrity world. We were surrounded by glamour and glitz and we felt like stars! We were all bursting with pride for Jane and there were lots of tears shed when she gave her speech. We had so much fun and it is a night that we will never forget.

I am so pleased that Jane has finally managed to write her book – it has been on her bucket list for a long time. It will be a bestseller before it even hits the shelves. When Jane speaks about her life in public her audience listens – there is no fear of anyone ever falling asleep. She has a powerful gift of being an excellent communicator. I am sure that Jane wishes that her story was not so tragic, but she knows that she needs to continue to share it to help secure the future of the LauraLynn House and to make sure it grows. Brendan will there in the wings, to support her as much as he can and the girls will continue to guide Jane in the right direction from above.

Thankfully, I know Jane will always remain a part of my life and I am very grateful that our friendship has withstood the test of time. We can look forward to growing old together! All my love and every success, Jane.

Fran O'Brien:

One day in 2005, I was working in the workroom. My sister, Mary Lucherini, and I operated an interior design business, Just Curtains Ltd., and at that time we were busy making curtains for a large order and had to finish by that evening. The radio was on in the background, and we could hear an odd interview or listen to some music, although generally we didn't catch the relevant details and had only a vague notion of what they were talking about on air. At that moment, the room was quiet, the phones didn't ring, and a soft voice penetrated my mind as I turned up a hem by hand, the fine needle held in my fingers. I continued a few more stitches, and then I stopped. My attention taken by what the woman was saying.

That was the first time I heard Jane McKenna speak. I was taken aback, and listened astonished as she described the tragic events which led to the loss of her and Brendan's only two daughters, Laura and Lynn. She described every nuance of their lives and I was very moved by their story. I heard then that she and Brendan had established the LauraLynn Foundation and had a dream of building a children's hospice in memory of their girls. While Jane never mentioned that she was fundraising as such it was obvious that a lot of money was going to be needed if their dream was to be realised. This was the first time I had heard mention of this, and immediately felt that I wanted to do something to help.

My husband, Arthur McGuinness, and I had often made donations to various charities, but neither of us had done anything specific for an individual charity. We worked hard in the company, and loved the theatre. When I was young I was involved in amateur drama, and although I had given up treading the boards, I still enjoyed the smell of the greasepaint. As well as the theatre, I spent my leisure time writing novels. Over the past few years I had sent them off to publishers in the hope of obtaining a publishing deal, but had no success. But I continued writing. It was my hobby and I loved it.

When I returned home from work that evening, I talked to Arthur, and together we decided to invest money to publish one of my novels. Hopefully, it would raise some funds for Jane and Brendan and the LauraLynn Foundation. But first I had to contact Jane. Of course, as usual, I hadn't heard any

Bunratty Castle, on Lynn's Make-a-Wish. I think this is a beautiful photo of our precious dying daughter.

Lynn in Barretstown on a summer camp for sick children in 2000. She loved BT, and would have stayed forever. Thanks Barretstown.

Me and Brendan in a rare romantic moment. He's had one or two!

Phil Dunne (CEO then), me, George Balmer (Chairman of the Board) and Miriam O' Callaghan at turning of the sod on LauraLynn House, September 2009.

LauraLynn House – September 2011

Brendan and me, receiving a beautiful gift of a painting of LauraLynn House on the day of opening. We cherish it very much.

President McAleese giving her speech on the day of the opening of LauraLynn House – 27 September 2011. I had to speak next – scary!

The President unveiling the Plaque, with me looking on – a very special moment in our lives.

Brendan and me on 27 September 2012 – LauraLynn's first birthday.

PJ, Kay, Pauline, me and Ann at Jigs 'n' Reels Charity fundraising event.
Sorcha Furlong (*Fair City*) took part for LauraLynn. She is a wonderful supporter.

Brendan and me in 2007, when I received a 'People of the Year' award.

Group photo of the 'People of the Year'.

Me and Pauline heading to one of the many Charity Balls through the years.

Me and my three brothers – Hugh, James and Maurice.

Lynn (10) and Laura (6 months) before Laura's first surgery – hard to tell she had a heart defect

numbers or emails mentioned on the radio programme so I rang RTÉ and tried to get her contact details. I was passed from one person to another and as I was very busy, I had to take a couple of minutes out of the day and remember to make that call. Which for me was some achievement, as generally personal things were put on the long finger and sometimes never happened. But finally, someone gave me Jane's telephone number.

I rang, unsure of Jane's response to my suggestion. Needless to say, she is a most beautiful person and welcomed my idea. Although, afterwards, she told me that she thought I was mad, and reckoned that she would never hear from me again. But that didn't happen. Arthur and I raided the bank account, established McGuinness Books and published that first novel, *The Married Woman*.

When Jane and I finally met on Grafton Street, it was wonderful, and I felt like she was another sister to me.

So the books were delivered. All 3,000 of them, which is a lot. I made contact with shops all around the country, and in June of that year Arthur and I would set off on a Saturday, a route planned out, and drive approximately 300 miles, and make ten or twelve drops to various cities and towns. Everyone was very interested, and all offered to stock a few copies.

That was the beginning. I had thought we would be burning the books actually and make nothing at all, but to our surprise we made a tidy sum for the LauraLynn Foundation. Then the following year, *The Liberated Woman* was published and we were off again. One day, Arthur was in town and passed by a courier company, Cyclone Couriers, and wondered whether they might be willing to give us a deal on delivering the books, as by now there was a lot of driving here and there around the country with repeat orders. To our utter shock, Cyclone Couriers offered to deliver and stock the books completely free of charge. In a matter of moments they had decided to do this wonderful thing for the LauraLynn Foundation. And Cyclone Couriers are still helping the LauraLynn.

So time went by and I published a new book every year. We distributed into the shops, and set our stall up at farmers' markets every weekend, and then we decided to participate in the Ploughing Championships. A small marquee was donated. And to our great relief the weather was good. And that's when we realised how many books could be sold at a show of that size. We were on our way. Now we take part in about fourteen shows a year, mostly in the RDS in Dublin. And there are some organisers who will give us a free stand, and others who give us a discounted price, for which we are very grateful. Also, Southside Storage came on board last year to help as well, and we also appreciate their help very much. This year we will publish the ninth book, *The Passionate Woman*, and also will reprint a book written by my Granduncle, Liam Ó Briain, in 1951. He wrote this book about his experiences in the College of Surgeons in Easter Week, 1916. He was a Professor of Romance Languages in Galway University for many years, and wrote his book in the Irish language. We will publish it in Irish with an English translation, and it will also raise funds for LauraLynn.

In 2011, LauraLynn House was opened at the Children's Sunshine Home in Foxrock, Dublin. We were very glad to be able to make the curtains for the hospice, and were delighted to receive products free of charge from some of our suppliers.

That day LauraLynn Children's Hospice opened was a wonderful moment for Jane and Brendan. Their dream had come true. For us, knowing Jane and Brendan has changed our lives, and we will always value their love and friendship. It has been a wonderful journey and we hope to continue raising funds for LauraLynn in the future.

Maeve O'Donoghue:

In February 2003, in discussion with my senior drama students as to who would be the beneficiary of our Annual Drama Showcase that year, Emma Manley suggested LauraLynn. At that time I knew nothing of the background story but through Emma, I got in touch with Jane, and that is where my journey with LauraLynn began. My husband Michael and I are now privileged to call Jane and her husband Brendan our friends.

To hear Jane and Brendan's story about the loss of their two beautiful daughters is heart-wrenching but then to hear that they had the selflessness, the courage, the dedication and the strength, in the midst of their enormous grief, to reach out to help parents of terminally ill children and work to find a way to make their lives and the lives of their children more bearable was truly inspiring.

Jane was always insistent that LauraLynn House would not be a 'hospital' but rather a 'home from home' for the children and parents who would find comfort there. Anyone who has seen LauraLynn House, which really is a 'home from home', will realise that it is exactly that – a lovely bright, colourful, cheerful home with all the medical necessities very carefully camouflaged and the Butterfly Suite a little oasis of calm and serenity for that final journey.

Jane worked tirelessly to achieve her goal and it was always a priority for her to thank each and every one who contributed to the charity with a personal letter and whenever possible took the time to visit to say that personal thank you. She travelled to so many schools, sports clubs, ladies clubs, concerts, fashion shows, garden fetes etc. to do that, and each time I listened to Jane's story – told without any sense of self-pity – I never ceased to be very deeply moved. When speaking to groups of school children Jane always had a lovely way of explaining what had happened to her girls and always managed to get her message across in a very positive way – the emphasis being on how they were helping to achieve this great goal. Her genuine gratitude and appreciation for every donation – regardless of the amount – played no small part in realising her dream and was part of the key to her success. On one occasion we visited a Ladies Club to receive a donation of around €25.00 and the ladies there, hearing the story for the first time, were very touched. They spread the word about LauraLynn so successfully among their children and grandchildren that it resulted in donations of hundreds of thousands of euro to the charity, and it all began with that €25.00!

I know that any time Jane has a big decision to make she seeks the help and advice of 'the girls', Laura and Lynn, and while they may be physically absent from this life they are a constant force in Jane and Brendan's lives and their abiding love and guidance are there with them always and forever.

LauraLynn House is a wonderful and most fitting tribute to Jane, Brendan, Laura and Lynn McKenna. My huge admiration for them knows no bounds.

Ann Tomlin:

I first met Jane and Lynn at a fashion show in aid of Our Lady's Children's Hospital; my friend Steve was performing so I went along to support him. Steve was great but Lynn was amazing. She wasn't long out of treatment and there she was modelling on the catwalk. I was so impressed and thought she was so brave. She also looked absolutely beautiful and was enjoying every second of it.

Later on, Steve introduced me to Jane and Lynn. Lynn mentioned that when she was better she would like to work in the catering industry, which is where I come from. So I told her whenever she felt up to it she could come to work with me on functions in the Honorable Society of Kings Inns. Not long after she called and asked if she could work.

Brendan would drive Lynn to work in the morning and collect her in the evening. I told her to let me know when she was tired and if she needed to go home, but she was enjoying it so much we nearly had to drag her out of the place. She was a great little worker and I think she liked getting the few bob too. Unfortunately, she got sick again and could not work any longer.

My husband Shane and I have become close friends with Jane and Brendan over the years. We often talk about Lynn's all too short career in the catering industry and how much she liked it. It's a tough industry to be in, but knowing Lynn and all she went through in her short life, I know she would have had the stamina to survive it and be very successful too. Life is full of what-ifs, so we will never know, but I am sure that whatever path she would have chosen she would have made an impression on everyone she met.

I am full of admiration for what Jane and Brendan have achieved in Laura and Lynn's name, and now know where Lynn's work ethics and determination came from. As they say, she didn't lick it off a stone.

I have to say that being part of the LauraLynn Family has had a huge influence on my life. It has given me the opportunity to meet the most amazing, interesting, funny, kind, loyal and generous people. Fran and Arthur are two of the most hard working and loyal supporters; they tour the country selling their books in aid of the hospice and creating awareness for LauraLynn. They are relentless and I have so much admiration for them.

Along with lots of new friends I have done twelve Ladies' Marathons, initially with a group of eight and this has now risen to hundreds. I have been to fundraisers, small and large, and prior to each one Jane has expressed her concern at saying her few words. She never fails to deliver and speaks from her heart completely. She is such a genuine and brave person she touches everyone.

Above all, it is the everyday person, who through this recession has put their hands deep in their pockets to help LauraLynn. Once people hear the name LauraLynn, they want to help and they don't need convincing to lend their support.

I have also been privileged to meet some of the parents of the children who have benefited from the most incredible home from home that Jane and Brendan have created in Laura and Lynn's memory. They have told me how much it has helped their long journey. Long may it continue, and hopefully with the support and much needed funding from our Department of Health. This is the legacy that Jane and Brendan have created for their two daughters. They should be very proud.

9

Remembering Lynn

*'You whispered in a million hearts
and kissed their souls.'*

Siobhán (Sibhy) McMahon:

I met Lynn on my first day of school. My mam tells me that
when she asked how I got on and had I made any friends my
response was, 'there's a girl called Lynn and I want her to be
my best friend.' We became inseparable from then on. Every
summer was spent either at summer camps, in Skibbereen
in West Cork, Spain or the Gaeltacht in Cul Aodh. Seeing
as we spent so much time going on trips it was such a great
opportunity to go on one last trip with Lynn thanks to the
Make-a-Wish foundation. Dromoland Castle was such an
experience, I will never forget it! Even then knowing it would
be her last holiday Lynn kept us all in stiches with her jokes
and hilarious observations. We spent so much time together
that we inadvertently developed a secret language – a look
or a glance would convey a raft of feelings or a simple joke.
Nothing more was ever needed for us to understand what
the other was saying.

I was always so proud to be Lynn's best friend. She was smart, witty, always ahead of the curve and in her dying months beyond her years in maturity and concern about the effect her death may have on others. Jane's work embodies her perfectly. Only Jane, who raised the two girls to be all that they were, would be able to create such an organisation that reflects them both and matches what the McKenna family was to me, a warm, caring family who accepted and looked after me like their own. I had many bright days with all four of them filled with laughter and love. Little Laura's health issues from birth never overshadowed her sense of fun and excitement.

When Lynn died it left a void in my life. When someone leaves your life you tend not to hear their name as much. Memories are the only things left and sadness about unfulfilled plans and dreams. The birth of the hospice however means I hear Lynn and Laura's name almost daily. Jane is an exceptional woman. Anyone can have an idea but it takes a special someone to make the idea come to fruition, not to mention doing so in the face of such tragedy and grief. In realising her vision, for me Jane filled the void. I see and hear Lynn and Laura everywhere, albeit in a different vein but one that is intrinsically connected with the comfort, care and security I felt from being Lynn's friend.

I am incredibly proud of Jane and what she has achieved. Dogged is never a word I would have previously associated with Jane – she is so gentle and soft spoken! – but in watching her journey since Laura and Lynn passed I can honestly say I know of no one more resolute or determined than she.

From the bottom of my heart I thank Jane and Brendan for everything they did for me as a child, teenager and for showing me in adulthood that anything can be accomplished if you believe in it and yourself ,and never give up or give in. The girls, I know, would be proud and in awe. I am.

Ciara O'Flynn:

The lovely Lynn!!!

What can I say about Lynn? Oh, so many positive lovely words spring to mind when I think of her. She was fun, brave, positive, caring, kind, intelligent, genuine and so inspiring.

I know Lynn since we were very young. My mum Carol and Lynn's mum Jane were friends first, and I suppose that's how our friendship started. We had such fun together as we grew up and Lynn was always a kind friend to me. I never remember her being hurtful or us having a row, I suppose we kind of just clicked.

I remember the excitement in us all but especially Lynn when we heard Jane was expecting Laura, a sibling for Lynn. She was delighted, we all were, and when little Laura arrived she loved her so much – that was what she was like, she adored her family and was very close to both her wonderful parents Jane and Brendan. Laura adored Lynn her 'Lynnie' and they were great together.

Lynn was so fun-loving. I have so many memories and I can still picture her laughing now. She was so much fun to be with. As young girls growing up we had a wonderful time pretending we were supermodels Claudia Schiffer and Cindy Crawford and that we were the girlfriends of some of the members of Boyzone!!!

When we were a bit older on a few occasions we were lucky enough to see Boyzone live in concert at what was the

Point Depot. We knew all the words to all their songs, and even some of the dance routines. I remember one concert in particular. Lynn was unwell at this time, she had been receiving her treatment, but she still came to the concert with her hat on and regardless of how unwell she must have been feeling she danced and sang throughout and we laughed so much that night.

Throughout all of Lynn's illness she never made me feel as if she was sick. She was so brave and strong and carried on trying to show you she was having fun and that she was okay!! She was remarkable for such a young girl.

There were times I remember we would be messing pretending we were the D'unbelievables doing the accents and laughing so much we could hardly finish our sentences. Towards the end Lynn was a Trojan, an unbelievably brave girl who never moaned as she tried to be strong and positive about things.

In her last few weeks we all really tried to have our smiles on and be there for Lynn – how she would have wanted us to be and that was having fun. I remember her asking my mum to make her famous chicken and broccoli bake, and then there was the party Lynn requested late one night where she wanted Pringles and ice cream. I remember sitting with her and listening to David Gray in concert in her Mum and Dad's bed and still now when the songs 'Babylon' or 'Sail Away with Me' come on the radio I think of Lynn, sometimes I hope she is giving me a little sign she's around watching us. There was the time she was going to Dromoland Castle for a few nights for her Make-a-Wish and the day a limo collected her as a surprise, for a fabulous day out, from other very special friends. We got pictures outside the limo and she loved it.

One big memory I have of Lynn's last few weeks springs to mind. One day she mentioned she would love to go in a fast car so it was to be arranged my Dad arrived a couple of days later in a Porsche Carrera 911. Lynn was delighted. She sat in the passenger seat with myself and my brother Ros in the back. Off we set up the motorway and she kept shouting for my Dad to drive faster, which he did. I was terrified but she loved it. It was such fun, and I still remember her looking back at me and laughing as she knew I was quite scared. At one point we were stopped in traffic outside a school and it was home time and my dad kept revving the engine and making funny faces. She loved this and was laughing hysterically, we all were. It was a great day and sadly that day was one of the last I was out with Lynn before she passed away. I'm so happy I have that memory with her.

Good friends are like stars: you don't always see them but you know they're always there. I suppose that sums up myself and Lynn's friendship. No matter how long it was since we had seen each other or when we would see each other again, it was never awkward. We would just get back to laughing about something or other – I knew she would always be there for me and I hope she felt the same about me. She was an amazing friend to have and I'm so thankful and lucky I got to have her as one of mine. She continues to this day to inspire me in so many ways, she had unbelievable courage and so much love to give and that laugh I will remember it always. Lynn and little Laura have such a special place in my heart and they will be forever remembered as two great girls who had so much love and laughter to give.

Aisling Sheils:

My first memories of Lynn are from her starting in Junior Infants and her first few years of school at North Dublin National School Project. I was a few years above her there and I always looked after the new Infant classes at break times while they got settled in. I had many 'pets' through each year but Lynn and three of her friends – Siobhán, Aisling and Ciara – will always stand out to me because they wouldn't actually let me take on anyone more important than them. They were with me until I left, particularly Lynn and Siobhán, who were responsible for their whole class screaming cheers while giving me a standing ovation at my graduation.

Others would call them my little ducklings, as they would follow me around the yard at break time. We had a Junior and a Senior yard and Juniors, for their first four years, were not allowed into the Senior yard, as it was safer and less chance of being knocked down by bigger kids. The four girls would wait on the line of the Junior yard that was not allowed to be crossed, and shout at me coming out of class. Of course I loved those little girls to pieces and they meant just as much to me, even then, as I did to them. I would play lots of games with them, hopscotch, singing and clapping games, and lots of imagination games they would dream up, mainly involving me being the mother/fairy godmother who generally kept them in line or granted them wishes.

As my Mum was the school principal it made it easier for me to keep up with them through my teen years. Many things stuck out for me with Lynn. I knew how much she loved her little sister Laura, and how devastated she was to lose her, and how concerned she was for her parents knowing that they would lose her too. She also lost her older friend Lorraine, who was also a schoolmate of mine, to leukaemia so we knew she was quite aware of what was coming with this diagnosis.

I was lucky enough to be able to see Lynn and her family not only in her last precious months, but also very close to what would be the end. Being around to hear her last wishes, hearing all about her Make-a-Wish, watching videos of her in her home, and seeing the wonderful last memories with her family and closest friends moved and touched me deeply, and was to have a greater impact on my life than I realised at the time. I remember thinking how much joy she brought to so many people, and even though it was such a difficult time, she did her best to give everyone those happy magical memories.

There was really nothing I wouldn't have done to help or save her, but obviously in the end it was out of all of our hands. Of course watching those close to her so upset was heartbreaking, and I was just searching for anything to do to help, so when Jane began talking about the LauraLynn Foundation she wanted to set up I was so glad to have something I could contribute to, as I know many others were. It was a huge help to allow many of us to be part of this who had felt helpless, as well as wanting to be part of such a great organisation. The first time Jane brought it up I literally felt that it called out to me. Here was this amazing woman who had lost both her precious daughters building something, from absolutely nothing, to benefit so many families. She became a huge inspiration to me, as to so many others. A couple of years ago I was representing Northern Ireland in an international pageant and when asked who inspired me most in my life the answer was easy – Jane.

Back when all of this began we had many weird and wonderful fund-raising ideas, big and small. I would do anything that was brought to my attention, from purchasing products where a percentage went to LauraLynn, to balls and marathons. And I also come up with anything that I could – at 19 I set up a Performing Arts school, which led to shows in national theatres so I would donate all our ticket sales and show profits. We had an annual Danceathon which the children loved and grew their awareness so some of them still contribute over 10 years on. I donated an hour's salary every week and encouraged others to give even once a month if possible. Before building commenced there was a fund-raising idea to buy a brick, with which you received a brick certificate. After requesting these bricks instead of other gifts for my birthdays, but particularly my 21st birthday and wedding, I could have wallpapered my house with LauraLynn brick paper! It sounds so simple and it is almost funny but it actually filled me with joy to look through the names on those certificates from time to time and see all the people I know who have been a small part of this and became aware of LauraLynn because of a small request of a €5 piece of paper. It was strange because a lot of people said it would get easier with the reality of a building and seeing it in action, and I never doubted that that day would come.

In the capacity of my career, both acting and my own businesses, I would raise as much awareness for LauraLynn as possible, anything I could attend and support I would. More recently, from bringing it across the Atlantic with a UNESCO charity award for work with several charities at an international pageant and still continuing some of the original fund-raising ideas that are now more like traditions for many of us, like the June women's Mini-Marathon. Whatever it may be, this past year out on the street selling stars and Santa hats, shaking buckets, or simply purchasing Christmas gifts at the online LauraLynn Christmas store, I don't see an end to it. My hope has always been to show people that you can always find a way to help, whatever way works for you. Seeing LauraLynn House as a real place was quite emotional for me. The first time I walked through the front entrance I was overcome with a sense of memories of years of efforts of so many making this now a reality. It really does live up to Jane's original wish of a place to put 'life in a child's day, not days in a child's life'. For these wonderful families at LauraLynn the amazing work there each and every day is everything to them.

After Lynn passed away Jane and Brendan became even more important to me and were involved in all my major life events. Not only because of Lynn, but also Laura, Jane, and Brendan, my life was changed and continues to be influenced. Before Lynn passed away I already liked volunteering my time for children who needed extra love and care, and I do believe that this would have happened anyway due to my own childhood with long periods of illness and my wonderful family upbringing. Sharing my love of reading with children is something that was already very important to me because it got me through my own childhood hospital stints, but because of Jane and Brendan, LauraLynn became a huge part of my life, because of Laura I began volunteering with heart kids, because of Lynn's Make-A-Wish I volunteered with chapters of Make-a-Wish. Wherever my travels took me for work, I found somewhere to volunteer in a way with children that somehow connected to Lynn.

Jane's strength influenced me to get through my own losses. Her compassion for others with less memories with their children and her gratitude for the years she did have with her girls continues to be a huge lesson for me. Every moment I spend with Jane and Brendan is added to the moments I treasure, be it sharing old stories or new, it always fills me with gratitude to be part of each other's lives.

Lynn was precious to so many people because she was truly not just a good, but a great person, loving to her family and friends, and full of joy and life. I hope my son will see these traits in me, because of knowing the McKenna's I try even harder to fill our life with as much happiness as possible. I am proud to have had Lynn as a friend for a part of my life, and now to call Jane and Brendan friends. After heartache and loss of my own, my little blessing was born early on Lynn's birthday this year, as if she was his very own guardian angel.

Sally Sheils:

Lynn started in the NDNSP in 1990. She was a quiet, serious looking girl who looked a little shy until she smiled. She had such an open, friendly smile – usually because she was sharing a piece of fun with friends – that you couldn't help but smile yourself. Lynn had a lovely way with all her classmates although, as a Junior Infant, she was sometimes less than enamoured with the behaviour of some of the boys in her class! This caused her Mum, in particular, much amusement.

Lynn inherited her Mum's gentle sense of humour and her Dad's more deadpan humour. Lynn loved doing jobs, bringing me the roll book, running messages etc. She also became great friends with my daughter Aisling who was four years her senior and who used to love minding Lynn and her friends. They all developed a lasting bond.

As Lynn got older she was quick to spot where help was needed and helped without being asked. Lynn was very loyal and she had a lovely cohort of friends – in particular Siobhán, Aisling and Ciara. She got on well with all her classmates and was very mindful of and kind to children in younger classes. She was such a friendly little girl and would happily stop for a chat. I loved chatting with Lynn as she was always full of the simple joys in life.

Lynn was an excellent student and always engaged enthusiastically with every area of the curriculum. She gave her all to everything that she did and always lived life to the full. She was so very lucky to have such balanced parents who could see the funny side of some of the incidents that arose for her over the years. They helped to build resilience in Lynn that was to stand her in good stead in future years. Lynn enjoyed primary school and seemed to feel very secure there. Her attendance was excellent which must have made her diagnosis all the more shocking for her parents. She found the transition to second level somewhat difficult but overcame the issues that arose and made more good friends there.

When Lynn's little sister Laura was born Lynn was thrilled and was such a very proud and happy big sister. She adored Laura and always seemed to have great fun with her. She had already built such skills helping with younger children in school that she was a delightful big sister. Her face would light up whenever she spoke about Laura and it was gorgeous to see such a lovely relationship and bond between them.

There were many reasons to be proud of Lynn over the years but when she faced her diagnosis her attitude was extraordinary and she really showed her amazing inner strength. Jane and Brendan have so proactively turned their tragic losses into a positive outcome for so many other parents and children that I am in no doubt as to where Lynn found her inner strength. Their absolute love, balanced, open approach and the spirituality they gave to Lynn gave her such a security that she faced what she knew would be a very difficult illness with a calmness and confidence that was truly inspiring and extraordinary. Lynn had such a love of family that she was determined to ensure that she lived the life she had left to the full.

Another past pupil of mine, Lorraine King, had suffered from exactly the same illness. Lorraine's Mum Dolores was such a close friend of Jane's that Lynn used to call Lorraine and her sister Gillian her cousins. Lynn had lived with her friend Lorraine's illness and death and she so admired Lorraine's attitude that she was determined to emulate her. She had seen the devotion of Gillian, Lorraine's sister, who had donated her bone marrow in order to give Lorraine a chance of recovery. She was deeply moved by their experience and she decided, in as far as possible, that she would control the illness rather than it controlling her. She started by shaving off her beautiful long hair before the leukemia caused it to fall out. She still looked not only beautiful but also managed to portray an unusual mix of serenity and mischief. She finished by planning her funeral – right down to writing a poem to be read at it. I keep this poem close at all times as it speaks to courage, love and hope and every aspect of how Lynn handled her illness speaks to the extraordinary bond between herself and her parents. In her death she insisted that all of us really cherish life and live it to the full. She certainly did this.

She had an extraordinary amount to deal with in that period with the death of her adored sister Laura coinciding with her own diagnosis.

I so admired Lynn for her selflessness throughout her illness. Jane and Brendan were amazing and supported Lynn so brilliantly that, despite her increasing tiredness, she managed to ensure her last weeks included many happy memories. Make-a-Wish foundation played a part in this and ensured that Lynn and her family had a wonderful break away together with friends. Jane and Brendan somehow found the energy to organise the realisation of other wishes and I believe that this determination to make every moment count made an enormous difference to them as a family. The videos that Jane and Brendan made of so many parts of Lynn and Laura's lives must be a huge comfort to them. I know I have certainly enjoyed watching them with Jane and Brendan who were kind enough to share them with me.

Jane and Brendan have shown such courage and selflessness in setting up the LauraLynn Foundation. They are an inspiration to us all. I had always known Jane as a quiet, self-deprecating person and I am certain that it took extraordinary courage for her to undertake the sort of public attention that was essential to the success of setting up the LauraLynn Hospice. It is also so inspirational the way she can tell the story of their family. It touches so many people and undoubtedly helps them through various difficult situations. Who could ever say 'no' to Jane who exudes honesty, commitment and empathy in every cell of her being. Brendan generally does not deal with the publicity but he has led and trained many young people in the mini-marathon and had no problem donning appropriate gear so that he, too, could run in the women's mini-marathon. The rounds of fundraising events that they attend for LauraLynn must be exhausting, yet they always do so with such good grace and genuine appreciation. I believe that very few people realise that all their time is given voluntarily and with love. Jane has, essentially, dedicated her life to the setting up of the LauraLynn Hospice and it is an extraordinary achievement. I know Lynn and Laura would be so proud of her.

So many of us come across tragedy in our lives, but very rarely do we have to cope with the loss of both our children. To see the lack of child-orientated hospice facilities for her own children, and then try to ensure that this does not happen to others, speaks to the extraordinary person that Jane is. She always claims to have been inspired by Lynn, but I know Lynn would say that her strength came from the love she was bathed in from her parents. They also imbued her with a certainty that she would be reunited with her beloved Laura.

There is something very special in watching a child grow from the age of four into the beautiful, loving, selfless and courageous person that Lynn was. I count myself so lucky to have been her Principal and I am definitely the better for having known and loved her. Jane and Brendan were so selfless and generous in allowing myself, my daughter Aisling and others to have been part of Lynn's last days. They will never know how much this meant. I have also been really proud of the way Aisling has done everything she could to promote LauraLynn and, just as Jane has inspired her, she has inspired young people she has taught to become involved in fundraising for LauraLynn also.

Jane and Brendan have always managed to make time for us and celebrate special times with us. Whereas this brings joy I know it also must be difficult to constantly be reminded of what they are missing, and their courage and positivity in this is also so typical of their inner strength and generosity of spirit. We so value having Jane and Brendan in our lives. Words can never adequately express my love and admiration for them and their beautiful and so special daughters Lynn and Laura.

Phil Cherry:

Dear Lynn (Lyndiloo),

I remember the first day I met you. You were four years old and it was your first day at school. You looked self-assured and seemed a little bemused at some of the tears that were flowing around you. My daughter Siobhán was in your class. When I collected her I was so excited to hear all about her first day at school. All she said was, 'I want Lynn to be my friend' and that was the beginning of a wonderful friendship.

Throughout the years that followed you were both inseparable together for all the milestones in your lives. What fun you both always had together. I particularly remember your rendition of the Spice Girls and you were the best Sporty Spice I have ever seen. Remember when you and Siobhán went to a fancy dress party dressed as Ab Fab? You were both absolutely fabulous as Edwina and Patsy. When Laura was born you began to spend more time with us as a family and sleepovers, weekends and holidays became regular events. You fitted in very well, not least because of your great appetite and love of food!

What I particularly loved was our trips to West Cork. I drove and you two girls tolerated Christy Moore and Mary Black and I sang along to the Spice Girls and Boyzone. We had plans. One day you girls would be in the front driving and I would be a happy passenger – alas it wasn't to be.

Do you remember being allowed to serve behind the shop counter in Levi's pub in Ballydehob? There were never many customers and I used to buy from you both. One of my most treasured pictures is of you and Siobhán age 7, then age 12, sitting behind the counter. I remember saying to you both that when you were 21 we would come back and get a third photo – alas it wasn't to be.

When you became ill, how sad and upset we all were. But what a warrior you turned out to be. I really admired your spirit throughout your illness – you were stoic, accepting, courageous and I never once heard you complain. As a young lady you were an example to us adults about how to deal with adversities in our lives. You gave us strength. How unselfish you were.

Well Lynn, you would be so proud of your Mam and Dad. They are such an example of how they have turned an immense tragedy in their lives into a gift for other children and their families. You would love LauraLynn House. It is a bright, happy place that offers so much comfort to children and their families at such sad times in their lives. What a lovely legacy Jane and Brendan have created in yours and Laura's memory.

Well, Lyndiloo, our Sibhy is all grown up now. She will be 30 this December! I do wonder what you would be like now – we both agree you would have been an accountant and would be driving a big car!

I miss you lots Lynn. You were very much my 'other girl' and I know you knew that. Thank you for all the wonderful memories.

Lyndiloo we love you.

Love Phil. X

P.S. Give Laura a big hug from us all.

Hollie Ryan:

In the year 1998, I began secondary school in St. Dominic's College, Cabra. Kim Lawlor, Linda Kenny and I had been friends before starting secondary school but we ended up in different classes. It was through popping in to them at break times and having some classes with students from their class that I got to know Fiona Kelsh, and also Lynn.

When we were in second year, we had all been told that Lynn was sick. We had also been told that her sister Laura had passed away. Lynn was in and out of school due to being ill, but on the days she was in, there was never a complaint from her. I specifically remember in music class, we had a new teacher that asked Lynn to take her hat off. To which she replied, 'I'm allowed to wear it'. The rest of us in the class were fairly angry with the teacher, giving out to her, but not Lynn.

I remember hearing that Lynn's health had deteriorated. Shortly after, Lynn died. At the age of 15, this was so hard to comprehend. I remember Kim calling to my house and breaking the news. It was a very sad and emotional time. Even though Lynn had died, she was never forgotten. In school we had our own Mass for those that didn't get a chance to say goodbye and students planted a tree in her memory.

Over the years different people did different things to help fundraise for LauraLynn House. In 2012 Kim, Linda and I organised the 'LauraLynn Charity Ball' in aid of LauraLynn House. With the help of friends, family and former classmates such as Fiona, the night was extremely successful. Even though the event was 11 years after her death, it was still a very emotional night and the feelings still felt fresh. The ball was not only a success financially, it created awareness for the charity to those who did not know the full story of LauraLynn House or the fantastic work that they do. I like to think Lynn brought us all together to do that, as some of us from school had not crossed paths for a number of years. It was good to see some teachers too. From the LauraLynn Charity Ball, many family and friends chose to fundraise for LauraLynn House. Many took part in the mini-marathon and also the Runamuck Challenge, to name a few.

The story of LauraLynn House will forever be a part of me. Jane and Brendan McKenna are remarkable people for achieving what they have, and for also letting those who knew Laura and Lynn be part of their legacy.

Extracts from Book of Memories of Lynn's Classmates

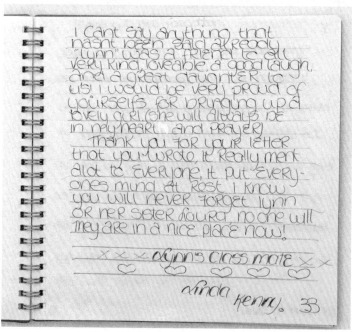

I Cant say anything that
hasnt been said already
"Lynn" was a friend to all
very kind, loveable, a good laugh,
and a great daughter to
us! I would be very proud of
yourselfs for bringing up a
lovely girl. (she will always be
in my heart and prayer)
    Thank you for your letter
that you wrote, it really ment
alot to everyone, it put "everyones mind at rest I know
you will never forget lynn
or her sister laura, no one will
they are in a nice place now!
    x x x o{lynn's class mate} x x
      ♡   ♡   ♡   ♡   ♡
        linda kenny. 33

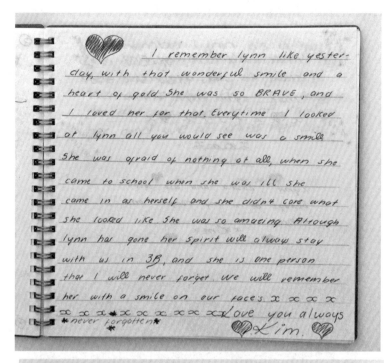

I remember lynn like yesterday, with that wonderful smile and a heart of gold She was so BRAVE, and I loved her for that. Everytime I looked at lynn all you would see was a smile She was afraid of nothing at all, when she came to school when she was ill she came in as herself and she didn't care what she looked like She was so amazing. Although lynn has gone her spirit will always stay with us in 3B, and she is one person that I will never forget. We will remember her with a smile on our faces. x x x x x x x x x x x x x x Love you always *never forgotten* ♥ Kim. ♥

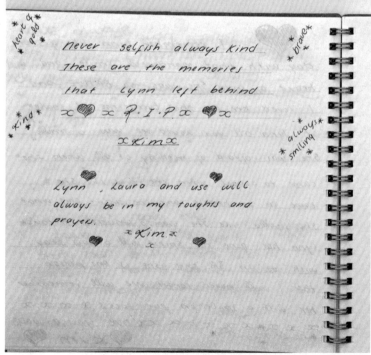

heart of gold *brave*

Never selfish always kind
These are the memories
that Lynn left behind
x ♥ x R.I.P. x ♥ x

x Kim x

kind *always smiling*

Lynn, Laura and use will always be in my toughts and prayers. x Kim x
x

I am a tiny angel
I'm smaller than your thumb:
I live in people's pockets
That's where I have my fun
I don't suppose you've seen me,
I'm too tiny to detect:
Though I'm with you all the Time,
I doubt we've ever met.

Before I was an Angel...
I was a fairy in a flower:
God, Himself, hand-picked me,
And gave me Angel power.

Now God has many Angels That He trains in Angel pools:
We become His eyes, and ears, and hands
We become His special tools.

And because God is so busy,
With way too much to do;
He said that my assignment
Is to keep close watch on you.

When He tucked me in your Pocket
He blessed you with Angel care;
Then told me to never leave you,
And I vowed always to be there.

I believe that Lynn is looking down on us now and saying
that to us. You brought up a very loving, caring, daughter,
sister and friend. We all miss her very much but we
know that she is happy with Laura and her angels
Love
Fiona.

I just want to say that you as Lyn parents should
be really proud of her. I wasn't a really close friend to
Lyn but we were friends. I really admire her courage
and your courage as well. Lyn has taught me something
I will never forget - to live each day to the full. There
isn't a day that goes by that I don't think of her. She was
such a lovely girl and very honest. I know she would not
want everyone moping around so that is why I live everyday
to the full. I will never forget Lyn. I will always remember
her for her courage, bravery and strength and know that I
am a very lucky girl in every way especially for knowing
Lyn. I am glad I knew her

Love always
Donna Kelly

10

Other Stories of Love and Loss

'I hope I've wrapped many a family in tenderness
which is priceless, and lightenened them with my love.'

Sharon and Brian Thompson – Victoria

Painting a picture

The brush is swished across the canvas of our lives and finally a masterpiece is created. She is beautiful, perfect and has all her fingers and toes. We call our perfect baby Victoria Edith Thompson and are the happiest people in the world. We are a family. She is the princess of babies and gets showered with gifts, love and time. We have all to give her and all the time in the world to spend with her. The whole of our world know how much we wanted and needed Victoria.

The brush paints on and our life is busy but remains colourful and bright. Each day is a blessing and cherished. All who gaze upon her love her. Victoria goes everywhere with me and our dogs and she is the whole of her daddy's world.

Slowly, greyish tints appear and Victoria has bad days, bad periods of time where she is hard to settle and where she feeds strangely. Sometimes she is very peaceful, but other times I'm worried and I'm not sure why. Her life canvas seems heavy, for some reason.

Three-month checks come but she cries constantly. Life is very dark grey, but no one sees it other than us. She is still beautiful, especially when she smiles, and we long to make her laugh. She reaches for toys and is bright-eyed. She grows on and we christen her and have a princess of a day!

Almost as if a dark brushstroke hits the canvas - Victoria takes a turn for the worst and I have to admit I can't cope. She is waking at night and seems to be in pain somehow. Granny will fix the picture. However, we just have to hold her constantly in our arms and Victoria refuses her bottle totally, as if to say, 'Enough is enough, help me!'

Neither my birthplace's air nor her Granny, can fix the picture, or help her. Neither can GPs, kind nurses or consultants. Victoria now is in definite pain constantly. We sleep on the floor beside her, whenever her exhaustion gives her peace for a short while. A tube gives her feed and her symptoms get worse, rather than better. As parents, our world is upside down and the picture is very unclear and dark.

We fight to get her to Our Lady's Hospital in Crumlin, Dublin. For Victoria, every day is a battle to try to tell us what is wrong and how to help her. She fights on and all those who gaze at her, love her instantly. She has a power over all and tested the best of medical minds and medicines.

A large brushstroke muddies the entire canvas. A large hole is punched in it, as we lose our Princess slowly and doctors get the diagnosis Victoria knew was coming from when she was born. She has an incurable, untreatable condition that is degenerative. Her nerves are not covered. Victoria is in pain, like we told everyone, for months.

Our baby will die.

Knowing what it was didn't help her or us. A cocktail of drugs is needed now and she must be kept comfortable.

The painting stops and large dark splodges of paint block out any remaining colour. Tiredness, exhaustion and helplessness cannot exist yet. Victoria needs us. We depend on her nurses and doctors constantly and she receives the best possible care – we stay with her all the time. Our canvases are empty and we try to patch hers. This is impossible. One hole appears as soon as another is patched.

Then, when we think the picture can't get any more twisted … we are told we will be taking Victoria home to Donegal. There is nothing they can do and we need to go home – that's what other good parents do…we needed to make memories. Memories of what?

Our baby in pain, dying a painful death at home? I was not angry until then.

Everyone loves home. We loved our home, but we did not need it. Victoria needed medical help, professional help and her condition changed constantly. I knew in my heart nothing could help her at home. We tried and failed to take her home.

Victoria ensured we had to return to Dublin. She led us to her haven and to the only place in the entire country that could help her and us - LauraLynn, Ireland's only children's hospice.

When we went to investigate LauraLynn for her, she gave us a very sure sign that she needed it. 'Bingo the Dog', one of her favourite tunes, echoed around its dayroom. We cried and knew this calm beautiful and safe place was for our baby. We knew when we drove her in the gates days later that she would die in this special place. We just didn't know how special our time there would be.

Our baby's canvas was now very small, full of holes and patches and dark splodges. To keep Victoria free from pain, we had to keep her canvas as stable as possible. Some days we managed it. Times during each day, we hope we added colour to it. Times it got damaged again and many times, a patch held things together.

LauraLynn staff helped us with the whole picture on Victoria's canvas. We were not alone. We had professional guidance and help. Our own canvases started to fill again with muted colours, but they weren't empty and damp. We added to the whole tapestry of life with Victoria there. Her extended family visited and she was held and kissed and photographed. Really lovely memories were made.

Her special Aunty Aishling visited every day. Her life canvas was cherished and although she was mostly unaware, she enriched the canvases of all those around her. We had time and energy to think of her and others. We had time to acknowledge and share our journey and accept its end, as best we could.

Victoria died at exactly nine months old, after three short months in her special home. We were looked after. We were not alone in our despair. The hell of losing our world slowly did not seem as lonely a road and we were supported. We didn't have to go home with a dying baby.

Our picture was as bright and pretty as possible and Victoria's canvas can live on.

Victoria has shown us that short lives are precious. That there are little to no supports for dying children in Ireland. She made us accept as best we could her condition and made us passionate about the need for funding and help for children such as her.

We are left with a memory of her canvas to cherish and work on. This canvas is painted on daily again. As no more holes can appear and the dark can be painted over somewhat, we hope that the canvas we make with Victoria now is as beautiful and wonderful as she would like it to be.

As Victoria lived and breathed in LauraLynn, she lay in her protected chrysalis and her wings became large and colourful. She broke free from her chrysalis, becoming our special butterfly. We buried her chrysalis as a shell for her pain now gone.

Butterflies have short and beautiful lives. They are fragile and precious. LauraLynn is the haven for emerging butterflies like Victoria. LauraLynn cradles fragile butterflies and all who love them. It gives them room and a safe place to learn to fly until they die. When they die the picture they painted over the canvas of this world lives on and is so beautiful.

LauraLynn helped our baby Victoria to be become a great colourful butterfly at peace. All fragile butterflies that need LauraLynn and a children's hospice should be able to be find shelter there. They should be protected and safe until their wings are strong enough – until they are ready to fly, fly higher than us all.

We love and miss you always Victoria.

I wrote this piece, shortly after Victoria died in June 2012. Victoria led us to LauraLynn, which was officially opened on the day she was born (27 September 2011). Until then, there would have been *nowhere* to help her. Since then, it is the *only* hospice to help children like Victoria.

When Jane McKenna asked me to include an extract in this book, I was so honoured. This piece was used in the TV documentary, *No Time to Die*, where LauraLynn is shown as a huge beacon of support for families. Remembervictoria9. wordpress.com is where I write extensively about LauraLynn and Victoria's life (and beyond).

Thank you Jane and Brendan. LauraLynn will be in our hearts forever. From all those who love Victoria.

Amy Cunningham – Miss Ellie

Ellie was born in the Coombe Hospital Dublin. A 3 lb 2oz little chick she was so tiny yet so perfect. But ... Miss Ellie was born with a rare condition called cytomegalovirus She was deaf/blind, with global development My perfect princess – my heart was broken! I was a young single Mammy at 20 and couldn't understand why me?

The next few days were a blur. Ellie may not live and was critical – I could lose my baby at any moment. We spent weeks in the Coombe, then on to Crumlin Hosiptal.

My Ellie was defying doctors and I was so proud she was such a warrior. My tiny warrior was really fighting this condition and after months, she was coming home.

Ellie was a determined, smart, funny, happy, sick child who never once complained. Her medication was like a small chemists shop and up to 20 syringes a day. As all hospitals and doctors link you to different services, we had so many, I actually couldn't keep up. One day a letter arrived from the Children's Sunshine Home requesting to meet us. Two lovely ladies called and told us all about the service. I was totally against it, as this was respite, a place to bring Miss Ellie to, for breaks. I was her Mam and I didn't need help. I ... or so I thought!

I reluctantly relented and we arrived at the CSH. I cried and cried and felt like I was giving my baby up forever. A nurse told me gently that while you feel you may not need us right now, think of down the line. It was a few days break to recharge my batteries so I could mind and protect her and be stronger! Having a sick terminal child is 24 hour care is so hard!

CSH was a huge part of our lives and became our 'home from home' for most of Ellie's life. It was very special to us, and was a very happy place which Ellie loved so much. Things changed as years passed, and CSH merged with LauraLynn Foundation.

On the 27 September 2011, LauraLynn House opened its doors. This house was magical,with its bright colours and wonderful facilities. It was Ireland's first Children's Hospice. Lauralynn House answered my prayers. A beautiful setting with amazing nurses and care team, it was our second home forever.

Our dreaded place became our true lifeline. It gave me a chance to be Amy again, and a Mammy as well as a carer. The nurses looked after Ellie just as good as Mama and I needed to accept that... From Christmas to Family days to Halloween and Summer days, we made such special memories I treasure forever. LauraLynn House, founded by my biggest inspiration, Jane, who amidst the grief of losing both daughters Laura and

Lynn had the strength to take a dream and make it reality. Trying to organise a fundraiser for a charity for one night alone, and this lady built a hospice for sick dying children to pass away with such dignity. You, Jane are my hero. Miss Ellie's happy journey with LauraLynn was something words will never describe.

The last room on the left hand side of the corridor which every family dreaded is called the 'Butterfly Suite' where the precious little ones lay in their final rest when they pass away.

On 24 August 2014, at LauraLynn family fun 'Zoo' themed day, Ellie started on the end of her journey surrounded by her favourite people in her favourite place. It was to be in LauraLynn where I would say goodbye to my warrior.

Okay, so Mama needs a plan! I wanted Miss Ellie to pass away like a princess. I ordered the flowers from the florist, pink Gerberas, our favourite. Pink balloons, fairy lights, butterflies and a big bed. We had to make the decision to leave the bedroom and head to the Butterfly Suite – a room I never wanted to go to, but I needed to do this to make her passing precious.

We moved to 'Butterfly' on Sunday and reality hit hard. I would leave this room without my baby. This room was the nicest most special room in the whole building and had a feeling about it that I just loved. We had family and friends call to say goodbye, and it was quiet, peaceful, sad yet happy, but just special the way it should be.

We had the pleasure of Jane calling to see Ellie on 5th September, and told Ellie, Laura and Lynn are waiting on you to fly high. It was an honour for us to have Jane on our journey right to the end.

That evening, at 7:05 pm, my beautiful warrior went to the Angels in my arms. My heart broke. Miss Ellie was waked in LauraLynn which was so special to us all. It was an honour and a privilege to be part of an amazing special place. Our LauraLynn journey does not stop here, as anything we do is for LauraLynn in Ellie's honour, to give something back, for what we received over the years. To only have one Children's Hospice in Ireland with so many terminally ill children is not enough. We as a country need more, so children can die with dignity and respect, as they deserve.

Our LauraLynn memories are something I treasure forever and if we hadn't had LauraLynn, I dread to think how I would have coped.

From me and my family, we salute you just as you saluted my Miss Ellie.

June and Joe Reynolds – Lucas

I remember the first time it was suggested to us that we might consider availing of respite care for our son Lucas. He was two years old at that time and his brother Joseph had only been born four months previously. The very thought of handing him over to be cared for by people we didn't even know sent a shiver down our spines. Like all parents, you think long and hard about getting your child minded in normal circumstances, but when your child has a severe brain injury from birth, cannot walk or talk, is visually impaired and needs round the clock care you decide pretty quickly that there is nobody that can take care of your child like you.

The two years since Lucas was born had been hard work, but we managed as best we could. Joe would give me a break when he came in from work each day and we would take the night shift in turns to ease the pressure on each other. Laura and Derek, Joe's two children from his first marriage, helped when they could but they were both still in school back then. I suppose it was shortly after Joseph was born that we took the decision that we needed help.

I will never forget the first time we brought Lucas to the Children's Sunshine Home for respite. It was a Sunday afternoon and we had agreed to bring him in for two hours. We drove out the gates with a lump in our throats unable to talk to each other for fear of crying and consumed with a mixture of guilt and fear for leaving our precious Lucas behind. Those first few times were the hardest even though we only availed of respite once every month or so. The two hours became an afternoon and the afternoon became a day and eventually the day became an overnight stay. I can honestly say that while the fear and guilt never quite went away it subsided significantly after the first six months.

Little did we know on that first Sunday afternoon that Lucas would become a regular guest of the Children's Sunshine Home/LauraLynn Children's Hospice over the course of the following eight years. Sometimes the words home and hospice paint a picture of a dull and drab building with grey walls and long lonely corridors, but this could not be further from the truth in LauraLynn. We found it a most warm and welcoming place full of bright colours and friendly faces. The staff are so professional and caring and very understanding about your expectations and requirements regarding the care of your child. Over the course of the eight years we came to know it as a 'home from home' for our darling Lucas.

Our journey over those eight years, while always challenging, was made considerably easier by the respite care made available to us. It became even more important to us after the birth of our third son Zach, when Lucas was five years old. If I could sum up in one sentence what respite meant to us I would say that it gave us back a life.

It is often the case when there is a child with special needs in the family that the siblings do not get the time and attention normally afforded to each child by their parents because of the care and attention required by a child with special needs. Respite allowed us to spend quality time with Laura, Derek, Joseph and Zach doing the things which other families take for granted but time that for us was precious. LauraLynn became an important part of the kids' lives. It was a place they were always happy to visit when we were bringing and collecting Lucas. They forged friendships with the staff, children, and siblings of the children in LauraLynn. The same can be said for myself and Joe. We have met staff and parents through LauraLynn that I am proud to say are friends for life.

Having a special needs child meant having to say no to a lot of events and formal occasions that normally a husband and wife or family would always attend. For example, a wedding in the family would be an occasion that all the extended family would look forward to and be in attendance. Before respite we would have had to decline such an invitation or one of us would have to stay at home to mind Lucas. Respite made it possible for us to be able to say yes to these events again. This is what I mean when I say it gave us back a life. Another example would be taking a holiday or even a short break. This would have been impossible to even consider before respite became available to us.

LauraLynn has been, and continues to be, a huge part of our social agenda as a family. We have attended numerous family day events and various functions over the years, all of which have been wonderful occasions and a great source of entertainment. Lucas has had the honour of meeting various personalities over the years, including the then Taoiseach Bertie Ahern and Miriam O'Callaghan among others. Our proudest moment was when on 27 September 2011 Lucas was asked to participate in the official opening of the new LauraLynn Children's Hospice. He had the great honour of presenting a beautiful picture to President Mary McAleese on the day.

The Kids have also benefited from Lucas's time at LauraLynn. Joseph was lucky enough to be chosen as a mascot for the match between Manchester United and a League of Ireland selection to officially open the new Aviva Stadium. They have also been very lucky to meet numerous sporting personalities, most notably Brian O'Driscoll.

Our darkest day was 27 November 2011 when at ten years of age our darling son Lucas passed away suddenly. I cannot begin to describe our pain at the loss of our son and how much we miss him every day of our lives. We brought him from the hospital that day to the beautiful Butterfly Suite in LauraLynn where we laid him out for two nights before his funeral. We were able to stay there as a family with him and our extended family and friends were able to visit us and comfort us during our darkest hours. It was a great source of comfort to us to be able to bring Lucas to LauraLynn and it allowed us to grieve in the peace and tranquillity of the beautiful surroundings of the Butterfly Suite. It made the pain of our terrible loss a little easier to bear if only for a few days.

We continue to attend as many functions and events as possible at the LauraLynn Children's Hospice and it continues to hold a special place in our hearts. I cannot thank enough all the staff and management we encountered over the eight years Lucas attended for respite. They will forever be in our thoughts and prayers and we are forever grateful for everything they did for us and our son Lucas. We shall continue to run our mini-marathons and half-marathons to raise funds for the LauraLynn Children's Hospice as a way of saying thanks for all you did for us.

Finally, to Jane and Brendan, thank you for finding the courage to keep going after the loss of your two beautiful daughters Laura and Lynn. What you have done in your daughters memory is beyond words and has helped so many families like ours to find a light at the end of a very dark tunnel. We are eternally grateful for what you have done for us.

Catherine and John McWade – Leo

Leo was born on the 29th of November about three minutes after his twin sister Molly. There had been some anxiety leading up to the birth as we had known since a 20 week scan and subsequently from Holles Street that he would arrive with a congenital heart problem, known as Hypoplastic Left Ventricle, where the left side of the heart does not develop correctly. We had been told that in all likelihood after surgery, a relatively normal life would be possible. This was very comforting to Catherine especially who was carrying our precious cargo. The pregnancy was normal and joyful.

However, when Leo was born, the level of concern in the delivery room was high, as he was a very sick baby. He was transferred to Crumlin Hospital shortly after his birth, and went straight into intensive care where, after a couple of emergency surgeries, we were given the devastating news that his heart condition was inoperable, and there were quite a few complications. One of the longest journeys of John's life was the drive from Crumlin to Holles Street to tell Catherine that their little boy was going to die in a matter of days or weeks at most, while she was busy being a new Mum to their baby girl.

We brought Leo home before Christmas, along with a barrage of medications, feeding tubes and other paraphernalia – all stuff that had been alien to us only a few weeks previously. Our living room had a few sad looking balloons, as people didn't know what to say to us – whether to congratulate or commiserate – it was a very surreal time. Our main lifeline at this point was the Jack and Jill organisation. They helped us in so many practical ways and provided nursing care for Leo to give us a break. Unfortunately, our poor boy was in immense pain and it became impossible for us to care for him at home. On one occasion we actually thought he was about to die. It was terrifying – we felt isolated.

Our biggest ambition for him was to see him smile, to be happy and pain-free, if only for a short while, and to have our new little family whole again. The list of health issues seemed endless and our inability to help him left us feeling helpless and wondering should the inevitable come sooner, for his sake. Things were grim to say the least. When we seemed to be at our lowest point, we got news that would completely change our journey with Leo. We were told about

LauraLynn, and after meeting with them in early February Leo was given a place there as an end of life palliative patient. That's really where Leo's story begins.

Leo moved into LauraLynn on 8 February 2012 and instead of his life ending there, a new one began – for our whole family. First of all, for us, having come from sleeping on a chair in an acute hospital situation to this absolute haven, it was an immediately calming experience. We were given a virtual hug by all the staff in the manner in which we entered LauraLynn. About ten professionals were sitting in Leo's new bedroom to greet us and they each explained their role and how their skills would help Leo. We were overwhelmed and reduced to tears by this. We weren't on our own anymore!

Things didn't change overnight. Leo was in immense pain a lot of the time for the first three months or so. The nurses and carers worked closely with us on a day to day basis, with the aim of keeping Leo pain-free.

There were a number of scares, or episodes as we called them, when he stopped breathing and his heart also stopped. The priest was called on one of these occasions to anoint him and texts were sent out that he had gone. But he came back – five times! We lived our lives through a breathing and sats monitor, waiting for the inevitable. Catherine slept beside him with his twin sister for what seemed like an eternity, refusing to budge – the staff at LauraLynn giving her not only support, but space to be his Mum.

There were many 'quick wins' the staff had with him, from balancing his feed and medications, to understanding how to keep him comfortable as he had very limited movement at the time. After a while, we had a little boy who began to smile for us. At first it was an occasional raise of an eyebrow, to a full blown face cracking grin. At the same time it was hard to believe that this little boy was living on a precipice every day. LauraLynn gave Leo back to us in the sense that we became the family we were supposed to be.

Leo lived in LauraLynn House full-time for a total of 11 months and part-time for another five.

LauraLynn was our home also. We lived upstairs in the family accommodation for a while. When we moved home (which is local) one of us would make sure to go up in the morning for when he awoke, then the other would come up later with Molly and we would play and 'hang out' in the day room.

During our time there, we were astonished by the dedication of the staff and the activities they came up with, from Teddy Bear picnics to beach parties to fantastic music classes, and the house was decorated from top to toe for every holiday like Halloween, Christmas etc. There was just such a happy atmosphere and it became contagious.

John generally settled Leo to sleep while Catherine took Molly home. There was always someone on the staff to talk to and they constantly checked in with us to see if we needed anything at all from them. Our own families also were part of LauraLynn and Catherine's sisters in particular settled Leo many nights and were there for the early morning wake up calls.

We were allowed to be parents of twins, from nappy-changing to trying to get them to snooze, the staff let us get on with it and just be a family.

Of course, as time went on, it became so difficult for Catherine to have to leave Leo in one home while Molly was in another – night times were so very hard. LauraLynn, together with Jack and Jill and other community organisations, all teamed together to help us bring Leo home.

This new phase of our journey was the most wonderful. We had him home maybe three to four nights a week, and LauraLynn and Jack and Jill helped out with the other nights. We were always with him during the day in any case.

Bedtime now was the way it was always meant to be. Two cots in our room. Two babies going to sleep … okay one had to be medicated every couple of hours but that was now 'normal' to us all. We all woke up together and early mornings playing on the bed with Catherine, while John walked the dogs was unforgettable. Leo adored his sister Molly and his eyes followed her every move. He pulled her hair, played with her toys and smiled every chance he got.

What had LauraLynn done for us really? We actually forgot that Leo was in palliative care … but they didn't!

Of course, the prognosis didn't change, but our outlook did, dramatically. We came up with a bucket list for him, so from the Botanic Gardens to regular swims or lazing with Mum and Dad under our Magnolia tree, our memories are punctuated with pieces of joy that we never expected to have.

Leo was with us for a total of 570 days. He passed away on 21 June 2013, just a few days after having spent a wonderful Father's Day with the family and giving his Daddy big smiles and cuddles.

The patience and endurance, the meticulous care, and not least the love that he got from everyone around him gave us more than we had ever expected or hoped for. Leo's lovely smile touched many more people than we expected due to a documentary called *No Time to Die*, much of which was filmed in LauraLynn. This documentary followed four families with a child in palliative care, one of whom was Leo. We wanted to take part in the filming as we felt it was vitally important to let people who have a child with a life-limiting illness know that there is such a place as this.

When Leo passed away in LauraLynn, Catherine slept with him in the beautiful Butterfly Room. She said a prayer to two beautiful girls called Laura and Lynn and their incredible Mummy and Daddy, Jane and Brendan, and thanked them so much for our 19 months together.

Even now, we feel that LauraLynn will always be part of our family. We will never be forgotten, we will never forget. Our visits usually take in a visit to the playground, and then the serenity garden, where we sat with Leo, where we release balloons for him, where we feel a sense of peace and calm, and are thankful LauraLynn exists.

Mary May – Hannah

After 14 years of marriage and six IVF attempts I finally became pregnant. There was huge celebrations as we had decided this was our last attempt with IVF. It had been a stressful and demanding process, so to hear the news I was pregnant was amazing. I was brimming from ear to ear. I, Mary May, was going to have a baby. I did not want to know the sex of the baby. I wanted a surprise and like every other mother, I did not mind what the sex of the child was, ONCE IT WAS HEALTHY.

My baby's due date was 13 February but unfortunately I did not have a good pregnancy. I suffered from preeclampsia. I was so unwell and spent many nights in hospital. At 25 weeks, I was given a medication to help open the baby's lungs. The doctors thought they would have to deliver the baby within the following few days because of the high risk of me having a stroke.

My health improved slightly over the next week, and thankfully I was able to hold out another five weeks. My blood pressure again elevated to the levels of stroke risk, so on 13 December 2005 my beautiful baby daughter Hannah was born. She was delivered by caesarean section weighing 3 lbs. She was rushed to I.C.U. but unfortunately she suffered two heart attacks and three strokes. Later that day she was transferred to Our Lady's Children's Hospital, Crumlin, where she needed special care.

On Christmas Eve 2005 we were given the devastating news that Hannah would never walk, talk, eat or even be able to take a bottle. We were also told that she was blind, but the one thing she did have was her hearing. We were devastated. I will never forget that Christmas, everything was dark and seemed to be in slow motion. We made it through and Hannah fought every minute of every day, so I became strong for her.

After ten days, Hannah was transferred back to the Coombe where I sat with her every day, all day long. After a few months we were allowed to take her home. This was very daunting for me. I had become a Mammy and a nurse overnight. Hannah now weighed only 6 lbs, and it was vital for me to learn how to place the tube through her nose and into her tummy in order for her to feed. Unfortunately, my marriage broke up shortly after Hannah came home. I moved in with my parents as Hannah needed 24-hour care and I just wasn't able to do it on my own. I had an amazing family around me, and this made all the difference.

I never thought I would meet someone again, as I was so wrapped up in Hannah's everyday care. I never had time to go out and socialise, but when Hannah was two years old, I went to a charity ball for children with brain injuries. Low and behold, I met Brian who was there supporting the same cause. I took my time before I introduced him to Hannah. As a Mam with a special needs child, you feel that nobody else could love or care for them the way you do. Brian stood up to the mark and loved Hannah unconditionally.

Life goes by so fast and time waits on no one. Hannah was now five years old and I had cared for her at home, with intermittent hospital stays. Epileptic seizures, pneumonia and other complications brought Hannah to Crumlin hospital at least on a monthly basis. Hannah was never left alone for one minute while she was in hospital. Around the clock, one of us remained at her bedside. In 2009, Hannah developed Swine Flu. She was on full life support in Temple Street ICU for six weeks. I was told then that her lungs were very weak, and that it would be her lungs that would let her down in the end.

My brother Ciaran and his fiancé decided to get married in Croatia. I immediately felt that I would not be able to go to their wedding. Hannah was at this stage taking 32 syringe doses of medication a day, three milk feeds through a PEG tube in her stomach, three nebulisers and suffering regular seizures each day. So how could I possibly make it to the wedding?

The Story of LauraLynn Begins...

I had been offered overnight respite care for Hannah at LauraLynn many times, but always refused. I honestly believed nobody could care for Hannah the way that I did. I wanted to go to this wedding so much, that I surprised myself and made the call to LauraLynn and they invited myself and Hannah down for a visit.

I will never forget driving through the gates of LauraLynn for the first time. I felt so much guilt inside. It was as if I was letting Hannah down by looking for somebody else to look after her. Driving back out the gates just one hour later, I knew that this was somewhere really special.

I can only describe a feeling of tranquillity and love. It was bright and airy, there was soft music, everybody was smiling. Even with so much underlying sadness there was a feeling of happiness. After filling them in on Hannah's medications, feeding and daily routine, I made the decision that I would go to the wedding and Hannah would stay at LauraLynn.

The weekend of the wedding arrived, and I checked Hannah in for her weekend away in her little hotel. Hannah didn't travel light that weekend – her suitcase was bigger than mine and it's a good job they don't weigh your luggage at LauraLynn. Her Nana Evelyn had a wonderful idea for me to buy a dictaphone, and for all of the family to be recorded, especially Grandad singing his ballads. These were her nursery rhymes.

The nurses at LauraLynn were so enthusiastic and impressed with the idea of the dictaphone as the familiar sounds would soothe Hannah in an instant. Looking back to Christmas Eve 2005, that moment when they told me that Hannah only had her hearing, I never realised what a gift that would be. Her beautiful, big smile would shine bright when she heard her Grandad sing.

I headed off to Croatia, but made hourly phone calls to make sure she was okay. Four days later, I picked her up and realised my little girl had SURVIVED. I was so proud of her.

This was a turning point for me. For the last five years, I had never availed of any respite care for Hannah. I felt refreshed and rested after my few days away, and realised that this experience had benefited both Hannah and me.

I gladly used the respite services at LauraLynn on a number of occasions over the last two years of Hannah's life. Sometimes, I would stay upstairs in the parents' accommodation. I would head off to the cinema in Dundrum knowing how well Hannah was being cared for, and pop in and give her a goodnight kiss. To see her peacefully asleep in bed just made me so happy that I could go upstairs and have a good night's sleep, knowing that someone else was going to do her 2.00 am and 6.00 am medications. It is impossible to put into words what this respite means to a Mam like me.

In late September 2013, I took Hannah on what was to be her last holiday with Nana Evelyn, Breda, Kay, Edel and Brian. Towards the end of this holiday, Hannah got very sick and was on oxygen for the last three days. On arriving home in Dublin, we went straight to Crumlin Hospital, where they told me Hannah was very ill. They made her as comfortable as possible, and were in constant contact with LauraLynn. I was told by the doctors what I already knew myself, that my little girl was gravely ill. They suggested transferring Hannah to LauraLynn for palliative care. I agreed. So the ambulance arrived and I went on that final journey knowing that the end was near.

Our stay at LauraLynn lasted four days. We had the most fantastic love, care and attention from each and every member of staff. They just glided in and out of Hannah's room, and were so respectful of all our wishes. We were allowed to have all the family there all of the time. Hannah seemed to be hanging on, so I told her it was okay to go, and to have fun in heaven and cycle that bike she never did. And run, jump and play as if there was no tomorrow. Twenty minutes later, my beautiful daughter Hannah passed away in my arms with all her family around her. And what were we all doing? Singing to Grandad's tune. It was so beautiful. All the people that loved her most were around her, singing her favourite songs. Nobody wants to pick a place for their child to die, but we could not have been in a better place than LauraLynn.

Shortly after Hannah passed, the nurses stepped in and when we returned to Hannah's room, she was all dressed in pink and more beautiful than ever. Yes, my daughter was gone forever, but so was her pain and suffering. In LauraLynn you always knew where the Butterfly Room was, but as a parent you never wanted to go there. This is a beautiful family room where Hannah was laid out with all her favourite things around her. Everything in the room is white, with butterflies everywhere. We stayed with Hannah that night, and the next morning had a short little service there. After the service, Massey's arrived to remove her to the house. They went above and beyond to make everything as dignified as possible. We followed Hannah's little white coffin to the gates of LauraLynn, where the staff had placed large and small butterflies everywhere. It was really beautiful. Grandad was singing Barney's 'I love you, you love me', we all joined in as we let off pink balloons for Hannah.

Everything we asked for was accommodated by the staff of LauraLynn in Hannah's final days and hours. Thank you to each and every one of you.

Olive and Des Tumulty – Katie

Katie was born nine weeks premature on 9 February 2010. She spent the first six months of her life in hospital with various medical complications and when she didn't improve as the doctors had hoped they started to investigate and she was then diagnosed with mitochondrial disorder. Katie had very low muscle tone (at age four she was unable to sit, stand or walk), renal failure, cardiac problems, was tube fed 24 hours a day, had developmental delay and was deaf. We were also told that her life expectancy was not good and that she may only live till the end of that year. The life we imagined for Katie of going to school and doing all the normal things was suddenly taken from us.

She did live to age four and we're so grateful for that time: we got to know her, and her cute little giggle, her gorgeous smile and we got to be a family together for those four precious years.

LauraLynn House

We had heard about LauraLynn Hospice but our idea of a hospice was a place for the very last few days of life so we never thought of it for Katie. It was a friend of Des' in work who mentioned it and said they provide respite also and if we wanted he could contact LauraLynn on our behalf which he kindly did. Two staff members came out to our house to meet us and tell us a bit about the hospice. It was very kind of them as I think if we had to go and meet them at the hospice initially it would have been too overwhelming too soon, and we might never have made an appointment to see it. We were able to get used to the idea that this might be somewhere that would be good for Katie and us.

Even though we knew that Katie was very ill and was never going to get better, we were devastated that Katie met the criteria to go there.

When we visited LauraLynn House with Katie (20 months) and Lily (3), the same staff who met us at our house showed us around the building and grounds and let us take it all in. It's only when you go there and see what it's like that you realise it's such a happy, colourful, friendly place, even though the reason for any child to be going there is ultimately so sad.

What struck us was that it had the best of the best for our precious Katie. The hospitals are so overstretched, nurses have to rush from child to child, and hospital rooms are so small.

In LauraLynn everywhere is so clean, fresh and modern and the rooms are decorated in such a nice way that are suitable for children of all ages. The bedrooms are spacious with all modern devices (touch screens that can be brought over the beds with TV, phone and internet). Each room opens out to the lovely garden. The wardrobes and adjustable beds look similar to what you would have at home giving the rooms a really homely feel.

What I really liked about Laura Lynn is that there is no set standard way of doing things; they look at each family and what is best for them and their child. For us we loved to stay and be close to Katie and this was possible as they have family bedrooms and a kitchen/living room upstairs.

It was brilliant as Katie was so well looked after. The nurses gave her her thirty daily doses of medicine and prepared Katie's feed which were given via her tube in her stomach (she was PEG fed at a very slow rate 24 hours a day). It meant we had a break from tracking her feeds and medicines as we did every day at home. In LauraLynn we were able to spend this time playing with her, cuddling her and having lots of fun.

The sensory bath was fabulous and was so big that for Katie it was like a swimming pool. Lily and I could be in with her and hold her without the need for a bath chair. Katie could get that feeling of floating in the warm water which she loved. The bath has speakers under the water and although Katie was deaf, she used to smile when the music was on as she could feel the gentle vibrations in the water, while she looked up at the coloured sparkly star lights on the ceiling!

The carers were brilliant, doing cooking with all the kids. Although most couldn't eat the finished product, they gave them the chocolate to touch, feel and smell and helped them stir the cake mixture with spoons. They always included Lily in activities and this was extra special for us as it was lovely for Katie and Lily to do fun things together.

Everyday there were different exciting things to do. They had an Easter egg hunt where all the children were brought around to find the Easter eggs with extra eggs hidden for the siblings too. We met many kind volunteers and groups during our stays there who came to help out and entertain the children. Katie met local beaver cub scouts who roasted marshmallows and sang songs. We met some celebrities in LauraLynn and it was good to be able to tell them how much the place meant to us personally and for them to see it for themselves. In turn they're able to reach out to a wide number of people to spread the word about LauraLynn which can result in more donations coming in.

One afternoon we took a trip to Brittas Bay with Lily. We left knowing that Katie was being well looked after while we were gone and when we got back exhausted, we were able to spend some time with Katie before heading to bed for a good night's sleep. I loved that any night we could stay with Katie in her bedroom as late as we wanted and if I woke up early in the morning I could pop down and bring her up to us in the family accommodation which we often did.

We celebrated Katie's second birthday there. Lily and I went on the Luas from LauraLynn into town and bought her some presents. Lily loved picking out a fabulous Minnie Mouse T-shirt that said '2' on it in the Disney Store. That evening Katie's cousins, aunties, uncles and grandparents came to celebrate her birthday. Chef Sally had made a fabulous cake and the staff decorated the room and got everything ready. We have lots of brilliant photos of Katie's party and it's lovely to remember her second birthday party in LauraLynn.

LauraLynn meant that we were able to have family holidays together. As my daughter Lily called it from our first visit there, 'the LauraLynn House Hotel' and that really is what it was to our family. We have so many happy memories from there and I'm so glad Katie got to spend time in this special place. She did lots of fun things – arts and crafts, games, sensory play, the list is endless. It's hard to put into words well enough to explain what an amazing place the LauraLynn House is. It's so essential for families with serious life-limiting and terminal illnesses. Life is so hard for them on a daily basis and LauraLynn gives them a break and time to rejuvenate.

Lily just loved going there and anticipated it excitedly like a holiday each time. We had the excitement (and stress) of packing bags and trying to remember everything we needed and then all getting in the car to go on our 'holiday'. On our last day Lily would often say, 'can we stay one more night?' and I'd have to say we'd come back again but that other families need it too and they'd be arriving later that day.

It's just such a special place. We'll be forever grateful to all staff who minded Katie (and were so kind to us as a family) and especially to Jane and Brendan too. We never thought that we'd ever need a place like LauraLynn but we are so glad that it was there for us and our family.

Katie's last stay in LauraLynn House was in February 2014. We didn't know it at the time as she was well but sadly at the beginning of March her kidneys deteriorated further and Katie's doctor told us there wasn't must time left and she died two weeks later at home with us on 13 March. During Katie's last stay she made a lovely Valentine 's Day card for us and she celebrated her fourth birthday there too. I'm so glad that Jane and Brendan were so kind and selfless in starting to fundraise for Ireland's first children's hospice all those years ago after the passing of their two beautiful daughters, Laura and Lynn. If it wasn't for them we wouldn't have had our very special holidays in Laura Lynn with Katie and all the happy memories of our time there.

We have visited LauraLynn a good few times since Katie passed away and they are always so welcoming to us. It's lovely that we can bring Lily back there as she loves showing her brother Ronan (who was born five weeks after Katie died) around LauraLynn and the playgrounds outside – it's great too that Ronan will know the place where his sister Katie had lots of fun times.

LauraLynn House helped us to be a family and do normal things; have a little break away, not to a hotel but to the 'Laura Lynn House Hotel', which gives families like us and their children a beautiful place to make magical memories that they can keep forever.

Sarah and Martin Gibson O'Hara – Martin

LauraLynn is a truly special place: beautiful, bright, happy safe, magical, fun-loving, full of treasured memories, adorable children with amazing people to care for them and give the children quality in their precious lives. On occasions of course, very sad too.

Martin was born 3 July 2010, a beautiful baby boy who changed our lives for the better, but due to lack of oxygen he suffered severe brain damage and his life prognosis was extremely poor. As parents we were devastated and we were told if he survived he would never walk, talk, eat, sit, stand or even breathe unassisted. Martin is tube-fed and is suctioned around the clock, sometimes for long periods. He is on oxygen constantly and struggles with seizures. Martin was four months old when he spent his first night at home, but returned to hospital 10 days later for surgery. Martin spent most of his first year in hospital. We had a visit from two members of staff from LauraLynn when Martin was only a few days old and they were a huge emotional support to us. After a long stay in Crumlin Hospital, Martin was transferred to LauraLynn before returning home.

Martin's first time to stay in LauraLynn was the day of the special opening ceremony in September 2011. A beautiful day and little did we know we were starting Martin on a new and wonderful journey in his short precious life. We were overwhelmed from the moment we pushed Martin through the doors in LauraLynn and we had no idea how much we as parents of Martin would depend on such a truly magical world here at LauraLynn. Both for Martin and for us, our lives changed for the better. When life presents you with a very sick child as a parent you will do anything in life to give your child the best of care. Now as parents you want to mind your child 24 hours every day, but after a while reality hits hard and you burn out. Well we consider ourselves lucky and you might ask Why? Because our son Martin is our most treasured gift we could ever be given and he has touched our hearts like we never imagined and touched the hearts of thousands and thousands of people all over Ireland.

LauraLynn, Ireland's only Children's Hospice, was like an answer to our prayers as it has allowed Martin not only to have non-stop nursing care during his stay, but also to be treated like the individual unique little boy that he is.

Martin is a truly amazing little boy – we call him our 'Superhero'. He is adorable, with his beautiful smile – a true fighter. He cannot cry but we know when he is in pain. LauraLynn gives Martin a whole new beautiful world, a world we could never have imagined with such dignity and respect and celebration of Martin's life, for how ever short it may be. A magical moment of care for Martin in LauraLynn was three years ago. I came to visit him and got a delicious smell of chocolate! Martin was helping make a chocolate cake. Now Martin can't sit up or eat, but the staff do their very best to create a normal environment, doing activities such as baking that most children love to do! LauraLynn has taught us to make each day of Martin's life a full, happy and memorable day.

The Arrival of Martin's Baby Brother

Spending time with Martin at LauraLynn when he was very sick also meant we got to meet other families in a similar situation to ourselves, and as parents that was a huge comfort There are many times in Martins life we're so grateful to LauraLynn, primarily with its special care of Martin and in turn minding us 'Parents'. When we made the decision to have another baby, we were comforted knowing that Martin would be cared for by the nurses and staff at LauraLynn during my stay at the maternity hospital. Martin was poorly when baby Patrick was five days old. He was slow to recover and I didn't want him to go to hospital. So it was wonderful that Marty, me and the baby could stay at parents' accommodation at LauraLynn. Crumlin would have been a nightmare!

We both really wanted Martin to be well enough to make it to our wedding in May 2015, and Martin was our ring bearer alongside his brother Patrick, and we will be forever grateful to LauraLynn for helping make this happen. Martin went to LauraLynn for respite the week of the wedding. Our big request this very special week was to mind Martin with extra TLC so he would be well enough for our special day. Our wish was granted and Martin managed some beautiful smiles and we were so proud and had the best day ever. Again, thanks to LauraLynn and the amazing team, we will be forever grateful. We planned a three night break in Cork and to visit a lifelong friend who couldn't make it to our wedding as she had just had a baby and our LauraLynn lifeline made this possible.

Meeting children of severe life-limiting disabilities and complex needs like our son Martin, and talking to other families in similar situations is a great source of comfort. If it wasn't for LauraLynn, I wouldn't be able to leave my home from Monday to Friday. Martin has had some truly special moments at LauraLynn – precious memories we will always hold dear to our hearts. We must say the highlight for us as parents of the gorgeous Martin, and I know Martin would agree with us for sure, is meeting and getting to know the wonderful, kind-hearted Jane McKenna, who is responsible for Martin's second home. LauraLynn House will forever be a special place in our hearts, remembering Jane and Brendan's two Beautiful Angels, Laura and Lynn.

Fiona and John Farrell – Daniel

The first time I heard about Lynn McKenna and her little sister Laura was in the spring of 2003. Our daughter Sophie was about four months old and was fast asleep in her rock-a-tot in the back of the car. We were out for a family drive and had stopped at a garage. I was sitting in the passenger seat when I noticed a bookmark with cartoons on it sticking out of the sun visor on the driver's side. John my husband had gone in to pay for petrol. I was curious and started to read the little bookmark. By the time John returned to the car I had tears in my eyes. The thought that Jane and Brendan McKenna had lost both their daughters was too unbearable to think about. How could someone go through that nightmare twice and still want to carry on, let alone want to build a hospice for sick children? Their story really touched me.

John had heard Jane on the radio a number of weeks earlier and was heartbroken by her story. Little did we realise then what a huge impact the LauraLynn Hospice would play in our own lives almost four years later. I often wonder if we were destined to meet Jane and Brendan McKenna, although I wish it had been under happier circumstances.

We experienced our own loss in June 2007 when our second child Daniel died in his sleep, aged 15 months. He had always been a big and healthy baby so when our precious little boy was snatched unexpectedly from us in the middle of the night, words cannot describe the total feeling of loss and emptiness. I don't remember a lot of what happened after we lost Daniel. Those first few months are a complete blur. I kept waiting for someone to say it was all a mistake and Daniel was alive. Still, we knew for Sophie's sake and ours we needed to do something to make sense of the horror of Daniel's death. While Crumlin Children's Hospital investigated the cause of Daniel's sudden death, we had the horrific task of organising his funeral. I don't know what kept us going, grief or a sense that this wasn't really happening, not to our happy little family.

Sophie was only four years old and she would hug both of us daily and say 'you still have me'. She so desperately wanted to fix it for her Mum and Dad. Most days I didn't even want to get out of bed, the house was so quite without Daniel – his cot, highchair, toys and clothes were constant reminders of our great lost. The reality that Daniel was gone and never coming back was starting to hit us hard, the pain and heartache was too much to bear.

In the week prior to Daniel's funeral, we visited the Children's Sunshine Home in Leopardstown. John and I had discussed that we didn't want flowers at Daniel's funeral, but would like people to make a donation to a children's charity instead. We met with Shirley, the Clinical Nurse Specialist there who showed us around, and introduced us to a little girl called Ciara who amongst other illnesses had cardiomyophy, the heart condition Daniel was eventually diagnosed with.

We decided to ask family and friends to donate to the Children's Sunshine Home instead of sending flowers. In the midst of all the sadness and misery, it felt like the right thing to do and we know our smiley happy little boy would want his Mum and Dad to do something worthwhile in his memory. At this stage we didn't realise the connection with Jane McKenna, only that terminally ill children and their families would benefit from the saddest day of our lives, and in some small way Daniel would be helping other sick children and their families.

After you lose someone you love, we all grieve for a period of time and then life must go on. John went back to work, although his heart wasn't in it. I on the other hand couldn't face it. I was inconsolable. All I wanted was my little boy back and no one could make that happen. I resigned from my job and concentrated on getting Sophie ready to start primary school. I didn't want to let her out of my sight; I was terrified something could suddenly happen to her too. Sophie's first day at school was emotional. So many toddlers in prams and yet no one knew we had only buried our beautiful boy two months earlier. I began to dread that regularly asked question: 'how many other children do you have?' How was I supposed to respond? I felt bad if I didn't mention Daniel.

It was around this time that John came home one day with an idea to do a collection of Christmas cards in memory of Daniel and donate any money raised to the Children's Sunshine Home, now renamed LauraLynn House. It gave us a focus, something we could do so that Daniel wouldn't be forgotten and to raise money for families facing the same horrific situation as us, losing their son or daughter. John began work on the first collection of the '12 Days of Christmas' cards for Daniel's heart! Everybody wanted to get involved. They didn't know how else to ease our grief and this gave them an opportunity to help. When John spread the word he needed designs for the 12 cards, lots of people from advertising agencies and design companies offered to contribute. A printing company agreed to print the cards for free and we even received the paper as a donation. The end product was a quirky and very individual collection of cards created by a talented group of designers. Every cent raised from the cards would go to the charity. Everyone we knew got on board to sell the cards. Friends organised coffee mornings, people sold them to work colleagues, family and friends. Our local shops were amazing, hanging posters and displaying Daniel's cards. The support we received was overwhelming and very comforting, especially coming up to another massive milestone without our beautiful little boy – Christmas!

Daniel's cards were a resounding success that first year and had the knock-on effect of encouraging people to raise money in memory of Daniel. Two work colleagues of John's set themselves a challenge to do the Cork Marathon, a stage of the Tour de France and climb Kilimanjaro, all in Daniel's name. They raised over €30,000 for the charity. In June over 30 ladies, mainly old school friends and work colleagues, did the mini-marathon again for Daniel – all money raised went to LauraLynn House. A total stranger, a Mum living in the area who had picked up a pack of Daniel's cards, contacted me and offered to organise an event to raise money in memory of Daniel. We arranged to meet for coffee. It was very emotional, but from there Daniel's Heart Christmas Fair was born. It's a lovely community day with people young and old working together to raise money for LauraLynn House. It's also a day that allows us to remember our wonderful little boy with friends and family, and I can honestly say it's a very special day and that everyone involved enjoys it, which I think Daniel would have loved.

In the midst of producing the cards, we also found out that we were expecting. This brought with it mixed emotions. We always planned to have a third child but it was an anxious time as we were terrified something would go wrong. Our wonderful son Matthew (meaning gift from God) arrived in 2008 and he and Sophie bring us so much happiness and help to keep their brother Daniel's memory alive.

In spring of 2008, just a few months before Daniel's first anniversary, we were invited to LauraLynn House to see the plans for the new hospice. We were finally going to meet Jane Mc Kenna. Even before we were introduced, we knew it was her. She radiated such warmth and sincerity. Yet this was the mother who had lost both her precious daughters and was devoting her energies selflessly to help build Ireland's first children's hospice. Jane and Brendan were such an inspiration to myself and John that day, we just had to continue to help fundraise for LauraLynn. Daniel's Heart Christmas cards are now in their ninth year. We never imagined how much would be raised in his name – almost €350,000 to date.

There is a very special sculpture that stands on the grounds of LauraLynn House to mark Daniel's contribution to the families there. It was designed by a very special artist, who I have known most of my life. When we asked her to create something that would in some way capture what Daniel meant to us, she came up with 'Sandcastles', warm and sunny, a constant reminder of the happiness we shared with him. We are so grateful to everyone who took part in the construction of 'Daniel's Sandcastles'. It's such a lovely tribute to our much loved little boy.

Daniel brought us so much happiness during his short life; you don't suddenly stop loving someone because they aren't physically here. I carried Daniel for nine blissful months, we celebrated his first birthday, we have treasured memories of holidays spent in Kerry and Eurodisney, fun-filled days out with friends and family. There isn't a day that goes by we don't think about him and wish he was still here. Daniel is and always will be a huge part of our family and we love when people remind us of little things he did when he was alive – he was so special.

'Sometimes a simple smile can make the rain stop.'

11

Further Tributes to Jane McKenna and LauraLynn House

*'If you hang on to the past, you die a little every day
– I would rather live a little each day.'*

Aideen Carroll:

Dear Jane and Brendan,

My daughter Muireann drove her helpers in front of her like a drover. Did she mention the church gate collections and spending Sundays counting the coins. In fact your efforts to build a children's hospice can be measured in the thousands of collection buckets around the country and yourself and Brendan's unwavering determination to keep it all going. Most of my LauraLynn memories are intertwined with Muireann, like the time she had a lunch party for all my work colleagues and cadged the ingredients from the local supermarket. It's not often they're asked to donate several dozen eggs, flour, mince, cream, strawberries and whatever you're having yourself to cook up a gorgeous lunch of Lasagna and Pavlova. The day was sunny, the wine flowed and the lunch in the back garden was a roaring success.

Then there was the enormous whiskey bottle that we trawled Dublin to find which was eventually tracked down at the Rathmines bottle bank. It sat on the canteen counter at work and was emptied regularly thanks to the generosity of my work colleagues.

Do you remember the flower sale we had in my tiny front garden? Advertising posters were plastered around the neighbourhood. Nobody knew this was illegal until we had a visit from the Corpo man that Saturday morning. His heart melted when he saw we were fundraising for LauraLynn and we were let off with a warning.

Speaking of flower sales, my sister Mary O'Brien volunteered her house and gardens for a really special 'Snowdrop Day'. With Spring peeping through, she threw open her doors and invited friends, neighbours and the wider gardening community. Working in the background were a host garden gnomes, in particular Robert Miller of Altamount Nursery, Assumpta Broomfield, Noreen Butler and the legion of cake and sandwich makers. The public expression of generosity on the day exceeded even our wildest expectations.

But the piece I remember most has a sad note. It involved an accident at work in which a man delivering a container of raw materials died when some of it accidentally tipped on top of him. It was a dreadful accident and very traumatic for the men who observed it and were unable to save him. As the material was no longer suitable for use, it had to be sold on. The proceeds of that sale went to the LauraLynn building fund so some small good came from such a dreadful calamity. May his soul rest in peace.

From time to time people enquired when would the LauraLynn hospice be built, but the day did come, and I remember you showing us around the superb finished and fitted building and gardens. You Jane and Brendan will be forever remembered in the hearts and minds of all those parents, past present and future, who benefit from this wonderful facility.

Muireann Carroll:

I first heard of the LauraLynn charity when attending a Dublin Gospel Choir event, where the warm up act mentioned he was fundraising for LauraLynn. I had done fundraising for many charities before and it was fortuitous timing that this stranger mentioned LauraLynn which allowed me to form a beautiful friendship with Jane & Brendan as well as creating both awareness and funding for LauraLynn Children's Hospice. I emailed Jane straight after the gig and the rest as they say is history.

I have many fond memories of my fundraising escapades. I wasn't flash with the cash myself and neither was the charity, although thankfully generosity soon started to come from many unexpected sources. So back in the earlier days of the charity I made homemade posters and charity t-shirts for all my helpers to wear, they were bright yellow and I drew the picture of the girls on the swing on each one. They weren't perfect but they made me feel more connected to the charity and were homely which I think is part of the spirit of LauraLynn.

There is great joy in giving and reflecting on how fortunate some of us are. Jane, Brendan, Laura and Lynn's bravery and love is an inspiration to us all. We climbed mountains, ran races, did many a pub quiz, cakes sales, plant sales, fashion shows, collections, bag packing.... You name it we did it and inspired others along the way. One of my favourite moments was bag packing in a well known supermarket. We were novices at this form of fundraising but wanted to give everything a go and arrived without collection buckets (our hearts were in the right place). Thankfully flower buckets were emptied out in the local florist and we set to work using our muscles and charm.

Myself and my husband did the Dublin Marathon in aid of LauraLynn, with pretty much no training. Amazingly we finished the race in pretty much last place seven hours later and we walked like cowboys for the week afterwards but it was worth it.

Another of my favourite and most humbling moments was visiting the Sunshine Home before the plans for LauraLynn had been finalised and seeing the great care being provided to such important, precious and loved children and young adults. It is truly wonderful to know that facilities and care has been enhanced for children and their families in very tough and often emotional circumstances.

Receiving a LauraLynn Christmas card from friends or family always makes me smile. When I hear Jane on the radio she fills me with awe and pride. Jane and Brendan have tremendous resilience, respect, love, compassion, selflessness and courage. They do their two beautiful angels proud everyday and it is my privilege to have met them and shared in the experience of fundraising for LauraLynn Children's Hospice.

Robyn Espey:

My relationship with LauraLynn began ten years ago whilst in Transition Year in Rathdown School when I headed up the school charity committee with my friend Sandra. We raised funds for numerous charities, however one that really caught my attention was LauraLynn. The fact that there was no Children's Hospice in Ireland at the time shocked me. My great aunt had passed away a few years previously in great care at a wonderful hospice and it saddened me that there was no such place for children. Jane's story really touched me and I began following the mounting stories involving the charity she set up.

In my final year in school SUCH (Students Unite for Children's Health) was set up by my teacher Chris Connelly and Rathdown pupils. It was a group that promoted charity work and fostered a sense of giving within the school community and ultimately raised money for childrens charities. Our charity of choice that first year was LauraLynn. We brainstormed many ideas and implemented many, but the two main fundraising activities included a CD and a fashion show. We recorded a CD, a rendition of Steve Winwood's 'Bring me a Higher Love'. I wouldn't put anyone under the anguish of listening to my singing voice and so, instead of singing, I threw myself into the promotion of the CD. I visited several radio stations early in the morning (with doughnuts) and got a few minutes airtime on each to talk about the LauraLynn charity and what Rathdown were doing to help. I spent my weekends in Tesco promoting and selling the CD. The CD was followed up a few months later with a successful Fashion Show in conjunction with CBC Monkstown, of which again all money donated went to LauraLynn to help build the hospice.

While I never personally met Jane through my school years, it wasn't until my Dad, David, was Class Captain of the Beneteau 31.7 sailing fleet, which race weekly in Dublin

Bay Sailing Club series, and he decided to do a charity event with a sailing theme, that we eventually met. He wanted to raise funds for a charity that would appeal to many, and so LauraLynn, both being local and a children's charity, was chosen between myself and my Mum and Dad, Jocelyn and David. I contacted LauraLynn to tell them of our plans and received back a most lovely e-mail from Jane herself.

The plan was to get the whole fleet of 15 boats involved in a race around Dublin Bay and Dalkey Island and have companies sponsor boats and bring out clients or employees for a day of sailing. The 40ft Challenge started off as a small event in 2009 raising €9,000, and after two years we were joined by the dynamic duo of Mark Compton and Cillian Meldon who helped raise the bar with the fundraising, helping it grow as the years went on until 2014, when after five years we raised a total of €100,000. The event carried on every year until the early hours of the morning with a full gourmet BBQ, live bands, DJ, raffle and prize giving. Everything down to the printing was sponsored by generous local businesses and every euro raised went directly to LauraLynn. Lynn and Laura looked after us every year with the weather, even one year when the gale force winds calmed down just in time for the race. Jane was very generous to join us every year at the event to support us, and although I tried my best every year to convince her to come out on the yacht race I could never tempt her sealegs.

It was great having the wish list provided by LauraLynn to choose how the money we raised was spent; this included beds, playground equiptment and parties.

When I was living in New Zealand Mum and Dad had the privilege of being invited by Jane to the grand opening of

LauraLynn House in September 2011 and saw for themselves what a fabulous place it was and where the money they had helped to raise had gone. I followed the positive press releases from the other side of the world. When Mum called me the next morning after the opening I had already watched youtube videos and saw for myself what a fabulous place it was. Mum even remarked how yet again the girls had looked after the weather for the day with the sun splitting the stones. She commented on how proud Lynn and Laura would have been on the remarkable achievement of Jane and Brendan opening LauraLynn House.

On my return from New Zealand, I spent every Sunday for 18 months volunteering at LauraLynn. I worked primarily at Willow View where they cared for older children, many with cerebal palsy. During my induction I was brought around to meet the children and found it was extremely tough and heartbreaking seeing children with life-limiting illnesses. Immediately, however, I could see that regardless of their illnesses, they were happy children living in a very happy and positive environment with so much love and support around them from the super staff.

I began reading to the children there and as I got to know each individual I would interact with them differently – some enjoyed bowling, some enjoyed getting their hands messy with paint while others loved to be taken out for a walk around the beautiful gardens. It was during these times when I got to know the children better and read through their personal books which gave a detailed insight into their preferences, hobbies and personal details, that they carried with them that it struck me that some were my age or not much younger. I left every week with a humbling attitude.

Like in all walks of life some people you will have a special relationship with, some more than others, and there were a few children there that I really looked forward to seeing every week. Whether it was the excited claps as I walked into the room, animated laughter or even just a brightness in their eyes when they couldn't communicate, it always made me smile and I in return hope that I brought some little joy and happiness into their lives.

I enjoyed attending their annual Christmas and Summer parties to which everyones families were invited. Seeing the children interact with their families at these parties made me realise just how important the staff and volunteers are at LauraLynn on a day-to-day basis with regular interaction being so vital to their comfort and well being.

LauraLynn really does have the most positive and loving staff. The children are always treated with utmost dignity and respect. It is not only the children themselves who benefit but the whole family because it is a wonderful place where families can spend valuable time together in a lovely, homely environment knowing their children are getting the best of care.

It has been my privilege to have been a very small part of LauraLynn in the past ten years and to watch it grow and develop into the wonderful place it is today. It has also been my honor to have gotten to know Jane so well over the years, a very special and inspiring woman whom I look up to and whom my Mum and I look upon as a very special friend.

Sibeal Conway:

LauraLynn and me

I have a vivid memory of my 10 year old self reading a newspaper article explaining both Jane McKenna's heartache and her vision of opening LauraLynn House in memory of her two beloved daughters. My mother, keen to filter the turmoil and cater for my young, naïve and innocent ears, read the piece for me in a watered down manner. Jane's story resonated with me from the first word, despite my youth and lack of life experience, and all I knew was that I wanted to do all that I could to help her. A couple of weeks later I held a talent show in the back garden of our humble holiday cottage in Lahinch, County Clare. Children and their parents from the nearby estate flocked to the fundraiser, and many local shops were kind enough to sponsor raffle prizes, despite LauraLynn not being anything but a hopeful wish, let alone a registered charity. My friends and I made £80 and were elated with our charity and organisational skills!

My mum sourced Jane and Brendan's home address and I sent a cheque along with a letter introducing myself to Jane and extending my sympathies and goodwill to her. Weeks later I received a letter in the post, a two-page, hand-written reply from Jane. That letter signifies so much now, reflecting on my journey with LauraLynn, and my relationship with Jane. It ignited a burning fire in my heart for fundraising, and thus, marked a sea change in my life.

In the years that followed my relationship with Jane continued to grow, as did my admiration for her and my passion for fundraising. Fundraising has taught me more about life than a lifetime of education has. The people I have met through LauraLynn house, such as the brave and courageous Jane and Brendan McKenna, the warm, caring and sympathetic chaplain, Thomas Begley, the strong and empowering former CEO Philomena Dunne, and the sea of friendly faces and friends and acquaintances alike who have surprised me time and time again with their interest and willingness to help and get involved with my fundraising ventures.

As with everything in life, some things are successes and some are failures, yet you learn so much from both. I have found that to be true with my fundraising efforts, however, the lessons I have learned from some perceived 'failures' have trumped apparent 'successes' in so many ways, and looking back, belong to some of my most fond and beloved memories.

This resonates more than ever looking back to 2007 and one of my first more 'official' fundraising ventures, a plant crèche in RDS over the duration of the Bloom gardening show. The concept behind the idea was nothing too exciting. I simply set up a service to have a 14-year-old girl babysit your plants as you spent the day at the gardening show. Looking back, as a much older and wiser (!) 22-year-old graduate, I think I could have foreseen that said venture wouldn't be winning any enterprising awards any time soon. Indeed, the crèche wasn't a huge success as hoped, however memories of said event will stay with me forever. My beloved late aunt, former best friend, and my long-time advocate and cheerleader, Richelle McCarthy, took on the role of 'fundraising liaison officer' that weekend and never left my side for the entirety of the long weekend. What I don't remember is feelings of failure and a longing to raise more money and have the fundraiser be more successful; instead, what I remember is copious amounts of tea throughout awkwardly long interludes in between sympathetic and kind hearted 'clients', laughs and conversation with my aunt which now make up my most cherished memories of her since her premature passing, feelings of pride and entitlement wearing the deep blue LauraLynn t-shirt, which fit more like a nightdress than a t-shirt on my 14-year-old self, and most of all, feelings of belonging and meaning, whatever amount of money raised from said event, albeit small, would go straight towards helping specific families, such as the McKennas, and in my mind that made for a more successful Saturday activity than what I had done every Saturday before then.

Such marked a change in my expectation for myself and what I wanted to do with my life. Anne Frank famously said, 'No one has ever become poor from giving', and that quote, combined with my enduring admiration for Jane McKenna, flicked a switch in my brain. Giving doesn't necessarily mean handing over all of your wealth and prized processions to somebody else; in fact, it's the contrary. To me, giving constitutes a range of actions, from literally giving someone in need money, shelter or food to figuratively offering part of yourself to someone or something that might need it. Lending part of yourself that might be of use – this might mean that as a singer you would serenade an elderly woman with a fervent passion for 1950s classics, that as a nurse you would offer medical advice to a worried and confused parent unaccustomed to intimidating and terrifying medical jargon, that as a baker you bake a sunny lemon cake for someone who might need an extra dose of comfort, that as a sympathetic person you offer support and love to a bereaved and heartbroken individual. We have all been blessed with a multitude of talents; how they manifest themselves, should they be overtly obvious or more introverted is irrelevant, what matters is how you use them.

We can all offer some part of ourselves to help others, and it is the grounding and inspiring generosity of talents and spirit I have witnessed first-hand over my affiliation with LauraLynn House that has given me more faith in mankind than I could ever possibly articulate.

Following on from the aforementioned realisation, LauraLynn continued to be a constant factor in my teenage, school years and more recently, throughout my life in university. From huge fundraising 'successes', such as 'Light it up for LauraLynn' held at the mansion house in December 2014, and seven consecutive years of carol singing on Grafton street each December, to less successful ventures, such as the aforementioned plant crèche, to incessantly badgering companies and businesses for promotion who didn't seem to be interested, LauraLynn House, and the effect Jane McKenna had on my former 10-year-old self, endured and is now without a doubt one of my the most significant relationships in my life thus far.

My relationship with Jane has completely altered my life, for the better. She is without a doubt the most inspirational, brave, courageous and thoughtful person I have ever had the absolute pleasure of knowing. I am so honoured to be able to call Jane a type of mother figure in my life. I don't know what I have done to deserve such blessing and luck as to have Jane as such a prominent figure in my life, but regardless, it is one relationship I never plan on letting slip.

I often feel that it isn't fair how I get to enjoy Laura and Lynn's beloved mother into my adult life, whereas tragically they weren't as lucky to be able to enter adulthood on this earth. It is, however, something that I don't take for granted. I imagine how Laura and Lynn would be today, had their lives not been cut short. I see Laura, as described as a Shirley Temple character by Jane, to be a blonde bombshell, now entering her twenties. Lynn I imagine to be similar to my sister Liadh, with whom she shares a birth year. I imagine them growing up together through their teens and into adulthood as my sister and I have, sharing clothes, advice, support and sisterly squabbles.

Even more blessed am I to have two supportive, loving and healthy parents. As the youngest of five children to a busy, working mother, and time spent alone with my mum is precious and coveted. My relationship with Jane has nourished my relationship with my own mother and now some of our fondest and most priceless memories shared together and time spent together are associated with LauraLynn house, and more specifically, Jane McKenna.

An apt quote to sum up Jane's journey and successful mission lies within a quote from the childhood stories of *Winnie the Pooh*: 'If there ever comes a day where we can't be together, keep me in your heart, I'll stay there forever'. That's exactly what Jane has done, honouring the lives of her two beautiful girls, a testament of the mother she was to them, the friend she is to so many, and the legacy she will leave.

Brian Fitzpatrick:

It is hard to believe I have had the privilege of knowing Jane McKenna for the past 13 years. Like all good things that have happened in my life, the influence of my Mam has never been too far away, none more so than my meeting Jane.

There is a particular group of people who unselfishly give their time and energy to raise funds for the blind. My first introduction to this generosity of spirit came when my youngest sister, Mena, was born blind. My Mam got involved in fundraising St Mary's School for the Visually Impaired on Merrion Road.

My Mam was typical of the people involved; while raising eight children, she always found time for St. Mary's. There were no egos involved, no fuss; just happy in the knowledge that every penny raised went to help the kids. When I first read about Jane and her girls back in 2003, I knew then I would like to see if I could help in any small way with Jane's vision to build a Children's Hospice. Once I showed my Mam the article, I knew she would not let me miss this opportunity.

I remember the day I first met Jane, for a number of reasons. It was Saturday, 22 November 2003. That afternoon the Rugby World Cup final between England and Australia went into extra time. This came close to causing me to miss a meeting that would change my life for the better, taking me on a privileged journey with a very special lady and her beautiful girls.

As I sat there in the Green Isle Hotel, Jane told me the story of the life and death of her two beautiful daughters, Laura and Lynn. We looked at photos, shared some tears and through it all I could not help but feel honored to be in the company of one very special lady. Jane read to me the beautiful words Lynn had written. We decided there and then to put these words on a bookmark and print copies for people to share and gain understanding of what a special girl Lynn was.

This was the start of my journey with Jane, Brendan, Lynn and Laura who have touched the hearts of all those lucky enough to have come in contact with them.

Thank you, Jane.

Peter Hanlon:

I first met Jane when she and Lynn attended a bereavement camp at Barretstown after Laura's death. My memories of Lynn from that week end are of a bright, articulate teenager who was trying her best to deal with the loss of her little sister while at the same time fighting to beat her illness. Soon after meeting Lynn however her condition deteriorated and sadly she died. The loss of both their daughters was pain beyond understanding and Jane and her husband Brendan began to live their lives without their precious girls.

During this time I met with Jane quite regularly and listened as she talked about trying to find how to make her way in a world that had suddenly become empty and meaningless. And yet despite her pain Jane was determined to make Laura and Lynn's short lives and deaths have a greater meaning and with that a journey of monumental significance began.

Both Brendan and Jane grieved as couples tend to do, differently, and yet despite the difference and Jane's slowly emerging public recognition they both played a huge part in the realisation of what is now Ireland's only Children's Hospice. My memories of sitting in Jane's kitchen hearing of her journeys to the U.K. to see how the Children's Hospice worked over there seem so far removed from what we now know as LauraLynn, but the commitment and determination of Jane to make a difference in the lives of other life limited children is startling. Her initial public request for support, the loving generous responses of so many, were all personally acknowledged and gratefully received regardless of amount. Jane's trips to schools to collect €100 were as important to her as those trips to the corporate world to collect much larger amounts. I regularly reminded her of the importance of taking care of herself and not overdoing it, but the job at hand took precedence over everything including herself.

One would imagine that to see someone work so tirelessly and selflessly would be commended by all, but unfortunately Jane soon discovered that although the work she did to ensure the availability of support for families facing the most cruel reality there were those who failed to treat her with the respect and admiration she deserved. And yet she never faltered, always set her sight on the goal and I suppose knew that along with Brendan she had two very powerful allies on her side and thankfully between the 'four of them' they defeated many foes.

Both Jane and Brendan have given hugely for the achievement they have orchestrated for others, first and foremost in the loss of their two beautiful daughters but also in their daily focus since the girls death to make LauraLynn happen. That goal has been achieved and it is incumbent for all of us to be aware of the high price that Brendan and Jane have paid in the service of others. It is indeed an honour to be asked to share a piece for this book because it gives an opportunity to honour these two very special people who managed to find a way to journey through every parent's hell, and despite their loss to use themselves to do something as precious as they have. It also allows all of us to remember and honour two very special girls, Laura and Lynn, and their short but precious lives.

Yvonne Lowry:

My journey with LauraLynn House started with a chance meeting with the wonderful and inspirational lady that is JaneMc Kenna in 2007. I attended a fiftieth birthday party of my husband Stuart's boss at the time, and he had made it clear he wanted no gifts but rather donations could be made to LauraLynn, a charity fundraising to build Ireland first Children's Hospice. I thought it was a lovely idea, but didn't really know the powerful story behind it until that night. I spent some time talking to Jane that evening and she told me her and Brendan's story, and the story of her two angels, Laura and Lynn. I was mother to a young child, and it really got to me! My heart broke for Jane at a loss that to me was unimaginable, and unbearable, and my admiration for her really inspired me to do something to support the massive undertaking which she had started! Her vision of a Children's Hospice in Ireland was very clear and needed a mammoth effort to come to fruition and I knew I had to do something to help.

I am co-teacher of the Carolan School of Irish Dancing and together with my sister Jennifer we decided that LauraLynn would be the official charity partner of our class. To begin we ran an annual Irish Dancing Feis for LauraLynn, which the parents and dancers of the school really got behind and it allowed us make a steady contribution on an annual basis. All our parents and dancers now know Laura and Lynn's story and are as passionate about fundraising for them as we are. The dancers have had such a fantastic time dancing at functions such as weddings and parties and have opted to donate the money raised to LauraLynn. Most of them have been out to visit LauraLynn house now, whether to present cheques, or to dance for the children at various events and consider it an honour to be associated with, and asked to be involved in such a fabulous place.

When Jane's dream finally became a reality and the doors of LauraLynn house opened in 2011 I realised that it was just the beginning and in receipt of no State funding the fundraising efforts required to run LauraLynn house were sure to have increased. I added a monster raffle to our dancing event in 2012, with a host of companies donating over 100 prizes in total, and first prize being a limousine ride, and tickets to Westlife's last concert in Croke Park the following summer. Lynn had been a massive fan, and Jane kindly donated some of the merchandise Lynn received when she met them years before.

In 2013, in addition to, and a week before our dancing event, I ran a white collar boxing event! Using all my contacts, friends and family to spread the word we ended up with 30 male and female volunteer boxers in training for six weeks and we had an LA-style production in the Wright Venue, full boxing ring, commentator, referee, the whole lot. The dedication these boxers put in in training in securing sponsorship, selling tickets to their family and friends for the night was fantastic!

The night itself was a superb success even if I did spend most of the night with my head in my hands as I couldn't stand to watch them all hitting each other! I was overwhelmed with the generosity of companies, some of whom I had already reached out to for the raffle in the last year, and new companies who gave us financial support, and products to help us raise money at the event. The brand of LauraLynn

House and the concept of the children's hospice certainly made my ask easier.

As a dance teacher I had been approached several times to take part in the latest fundraising craze *Strictly Come Dancing*. I knew it was something I would love to do, but I really wanted to do it for LauraLynn House. I had probably allowed just enough time to pass to soften my memory of the mammoth work in organising these events, and decided in July 2015 sure why not run one myself! So off I went again! Scouting for participants, sponsors, dancers trainers etc. Once again we had 30 participants 15 male and 15 female. This was a very different experience as I took part as a contestant along with my husband Stuart! I also had my mam, some of our dancers, and parents of dancers in our class taking part.

The six weeks training were scary, hilarious, and brilliant all at the same time! We had all levels of expertise from extremely good to oh dear! We learned a group routine and each couple had a routine also. Again, the dedication, hard work and fantastic attitude of the volunteer dancers (some might argue I volunteered them!) in securing sponsorship, and selling tickets, and working so hard to ensure that we had a fabulous show prepared for the night was nothing short of inspirational. And I also have to mention the support I received from endless companies and individuals was phenomenal.

The event itself was fantastic. Even if I do say so myself we put on a great show! Each and every dancer was amazing. We had the pleasure of having Jane and Brendan with us on the night along with some of their friends, and Jane kindly spoke to the audience which I know had a massive impact on them.

The Crowne Plaza Northwood was a spectacular venue, and the audience couldn't have been better.

The Carolan School of Dancing performed at the interval, and we finished the night off with a medley of dances led by Don, with all the *Strictly* dancers, and everyone in the audience taking part.

We raised lots of money and had the time of our lives!

I have met some wonderful people over the years though the work with LauraLynn, and have some lifelong friendships as a result. None of the events or fundraising efforts that I have been involved in would have been possible without the support of so many people. Firstly and most importantly my own amazing family, who never fail to row in and get behind each event. My large circle of friends, the parents and dancers of the Carolan School of Irish Dancing, my work colleagues in Enterprise Ireland, the volunteers who take part in the events and all the companies that have supported these event over the years make this all possible.

But lastly and by no means least, this all started with the amazing inspirational lady that is Jane McKenna. Without Jane giving selflessly by sharing and re-living her own tragedy, LauraLynn House wouldn't exist. Jane's vision for putting 'life into a child's day' really has come true in the haven that is LauraLynn House. A beautiful legacy to her beautiful girls.

Orlaith McCarthy:

I first came across Jane McKenna and her daughters Laura and Lynn, when my 10 year old daughter, Sibeal, was reading an article in the *Sunday Independent*. She asked me to finish reading it to her and as the story was so overwhelmingly sad, I hesitated as to whether or not I should continue. I am so grateful now that I did. That article started a lifelong relationship between my daughter and Jane.

Sibeal's reaction to the article was to immediately fundraise for what was then a dream of Jane's, to build the first Children's Hospice in Ireland. She put on a concert in the back garden and raised €82.00. She despatched this to Jane and Jane wrote a handwritten note of thanks to her. This formed the beginning of their relationship. I have always believed in the power of a handwritten thank-you note but nowhere has it been more in evidence than in Jane's fundraising for the children's' hospice. The handwritten note forms a bond between the fundraiser and the charity. On every occasion that funds were raised through the various concerts, collections, Mother's Day lunches and carol singing, Jane always wrote a note of thanks. She is now part of our lives as are Laura and Lynn. Charities can become largely impersonal organisations but in the case of the LauraLynn Hospice the charity has always remained very much identified with Laura and Lynn McKenna. It is the identity of Jane's children being attached to the charity that has led to the huge success and long term commitment of fundraisers. Large charities can become faceless and bureaucratic, however Jane has given the LauraLynn Hospice an identity that personifies the charity.

A large part of the fundraising success goes to raising the profile of the charity, there is a huge awareness of the Children's Hospice.

The construction of the Hospice brought out the best in everyone associated with it from brick layers to the landscapers who completed the gardens. It is a sanctuary of peace for those that visit.

Over the intervening 14 years, my daughter has gained so much more from her association with the Charity and with Jane than she will ever be able to give. She was lucky enough to enjoy through her childhood extremely good health. Unfortunately, there are many children that have long-term life-threatening illnesses. Laura, Lynn and Jane have ensured that they will have and enjoy the optimum quality of life that is possible.

Brendan and Jane turned their personal tragedy into a life line for Irish children and their parents. Brendan and Jane McKenna have showed the true power of love.

David Prendergast:

In memory of Beth

The date 19 July 2008 is seared on my soul. It was that day at 2.00 o'clock in the morning that my wife Kim and I lay next to our two and half year old daughter Beth in our bed at home, softly singing lullabies and kissing her as we watched her breathing slowly wind down and gradually taper away. I caught her last breath with my kiss as she died, and with that I took a little piece of her that stays with me and holds me steady in times of stress and worry.

I wish with all my heart that the preceding day had been as peaceful and pain-free as that final moment.

Let me back up however. Beth was diagnosed with a very rare form of Leukaemia at the end of November 2007 following several weeks of flu-like symptoms where nothing seemed to make her feel better. As our bouncy little toddler grew more listless, we were sent down to Temple Street Children's hospital where a lumbar puncture procedure confirmed our worst fears of cancer. An ambulance ride across to Crumlin

Children's hospital launched us into long months of tests, needles, chemotherapy, bustling schedules, small victories and major defeats, interspersed with many kindnesses from the wonderful staff and parents living on the ward. This maelstrom culminated in a long stay in the bone marrow unit where our five-year-old son Harry heroically donated some of his bone marrow to give his sister the best chance at life. By this point several courses of intensive chemotherapy had proven inadequate and we were informed that the bone marrow transplant would be our last chance as Beth's poor body could stand up to no more curative treatment. The long days dragged in the confines of the BMT unit but at the end of it she managed to walk out of the hospital and we were able to take her home for several lovely weeks filled with relatively normalcy, sunshine and laughter. Then one day the fevers returned.

Tests confirmed the worst that the cancer was back and nothing further could be done. Subdued meetings in drab rooms discussing options available to us and Beth in the immediate future, given that no Children's Hospice existed in Ireland at that time. We were told that we could return to the hospital ward if we wanted or we would receive excellent community palliative care support should we choose to take Beth home. By this time, Beth and Kim had spent seven out of the nine months since diagnosis stuck in a small shared room in a children's cancer ward. During that time we had seen several children die on the ward and there are no words to express how hard this is on everybody involved. The child and their family are in the equivalent of a goldfish bowl. The nurses and ward staff are trained to heal and cure, rather than provide palliative care, and they find it heartbreaking to see the children they have fought to save wither away. Other parents and children on the ward of course also know the little person 'in the death room at the end of the corridor'. Respectfully drawn curtains and muttered prayers from neighbours cannot drown away the sobs or indeed memory of the grieving father I saw insistently carrying the body of his young lad out of the ward to the morgue. 'There but for the grace of God, goes I (or my child)' the other parents think before returning to the daily rituals and battles of survival that make up life in this small sequestered corner of existence.

By the time our dreaded turn came to make this decision, Kim and I had already decided that we would take Beth home. We were assured that the best of care would be available and it possibly would have been under most circumstances. From the beginning we noticed some worrying issues such as a community palliative care nurse who had never worked with children, nor was qualified in the rapid delivery of pain relief though the Hickman catheter tube in Beth's chest.

We were told that no one knew how long Beth would last once treatment stopped. Six weeks was considered the outside limit. She lasted six days.

From the outset of our return home, Beth was given heavy doses of morphine. On the morning of day six she was wincing every time she was moved and by lunchtime she suddenly started screaming – viscerally screaming – for hours. I continue to hear its echo seven years later. Beth's grip on my hand was painful – a two-year-old hurting the hand of a grown man.

I will spare you the next few hours and just summarise that Beth suffered a ruptured spleen and that the emergency consultant who heard Beth's cries in the background as I spoke desperately to him over the phone, immediately left his duties and flew down the motorway to our house. Upon arriving this doctor was astonished that an amount of morphine that would render an adult male nearly unconscious had no more effect than to give her 15-20 minutes of relief. Brief blessed moments between the waves of pain. It was here that Beth served me her final cup of tea with her beloved play set. Eventually the doctor said he could keep the pain at bay no longer and we would need to sedate Beth with Ketamine; essentially putting her into a coma for the last few hours of her life.

This brought up the next problem. Where the hell do you get a powerful drug like this at 6.00 pm on a Friday evening in rural Ireland? Ketamine is not something you can buy off the shelf and the consultant's local hospital pharmacy had closed. It came down to me, the father of Beth having to take time away from her bedside to make a phone call to the cancer ward at the children's hospital in Dublin and ask them for help. The gods were with us that day as I caught the pharmacist on her way out of the door. She ran back and made up the dose needed and one of the amazing ward nurses jumped in a taxi and raced out to our house with a police escort. Once the anaesthesia was administered, our little girl went to sleep and slowly wound down over the course of the night.

I have to say the individuals and institutions involved were fantastic. For example, I have vague memories of our local GP racing hundreds of miles from his holiday in Clare in order to be with us at the end. Any failings were purely systemic – a result of not having 24-hour pharmacies, experienced paediatric palliative care teams and adequate training or resources to cope with the more unusual and extreme circumstances such as a ruptured spleen. A single Children's Hospice cannot fix this for an entire country but it can act as a centre of excellence, critiquing standards, providing training as well as front line services.

In my deep shock, this was the battle I identified and committed myself to during a conversation the next day on the phone with work colleague and friend from Intel, Eric Dishman. I'd imagine it was one of the more difficult conversations he has been in.

In the months to follow Kim and I initially began by raising some funds locally and eventually hooked up with Jane McKenna who was already some way along the same journey with her organisation LauraLynn. This began a wonderful collaboration with an amazing woman who for me symbolises the power of the ordinary person to become extraordinary under extreme pressure and to move mountains when the need is upon them.

Many of our friends and family do not live in Ireland so had not been able to help directly but it was heartening to see how people threw themselves into the struggle to raise funds and awareness for the hospice. Local people, schools and clubs supported campaign after campaign as we repeatedly tore open wounds to explain exactly why a Children's Hospice is essential. I work at Intel and my co-workers too were extraordinary, managers not only supporting my volunteering but acting as confidants and guides during some intense personal moments. Work colleagues who wanted to help my family personally – from turning up unexpectedly on a weekend to help us move house, providing taxi services, to reading the eulogy at Beth's funeral in my place. The list goes on. Louis Burns, my old General Manager in Intel's

Digital Health Group, rode a bicycle across America with a picture of Beth on his handlebars raising money for children's cancer research. And then there are the thousands of Intel employees in Ireland, Europe and America who supported the magnificent Intel Ireland Site Charity Committee, sponsored, rode, baked, walked, dressed up as clowns and gave money, time and their technical expertise to help build and future-proof Ireland's first and only Children's Hospice. It has been both an honour and a comfort watching these individuals and groups stand up to be counted alongside myself – and Beth.

You can imagine the mixed emotions watching the hospice move from architect plan to physical building and then finally a day of speeches, balloons and cameras when LauraLynn House was finally launched officially. The hospice will always hold an important place in the hearts of my family and I. To us it represents a support that did not exist when our daughter needed it the most, but it also represents ongoing charitable action by hundreds of thousands of people in Ireland and beyond to fill this appallingly shameful gap in public provision.

How are Kim, Harry and I doing in the years since Beth's death? Some days continue to be harder than others, but we have learned how to carry on during the dark times. We have been blessed with the birth of Kate and gradually we started to figure out how to smile again. Or perhaps allow ourselves permission to do so a little. We've also learned how much love and kindness there is around us. Ultimately, we are all just humans trying our best and we must remember to cherish the 'normal' moments in our lives – we take them for granted and then they are gone.

12

How You Can Help

'Giving and receiving love is the central fact of every living life.'

By finding strength in grief and turning it into giving, Jane McKenna is the inspiration behind LauraLynn, Ireland's Children's Hospice, which is a remarkable legacy to both her girls. Jane's story is one of tragedy but acts as inspiration to anyone who has lost a loved one. Jane is the heart and soul of LauraLynn and is always giving of her time and support to families and staff.

LauraLynn, Ireland's Children's Hospice, opened in September 2011 and cares for children with life-limiting conditions and their families, by providing transitional care, home support, respite, crisis and end-of-life care. Our approach is holistic, ensuring that the whole family is supported, allowing parents to be 'Mums and Dads' rather than full-time carers.

We need to raise in excess of €3 million every year to keep the doors of our Hospice open and to continue to provide our LauraLynn@HOME programme, which brings hands-on hospice care directly into the comfort of a child's home. As well as delivering our current Hospice care, we have been busy developing plans so that we can offer this much needed care to more children and families. We need your continued support to enable us to this.

Please check out our website, www.lauralynn.ie, for information on how you can help LauraLynn, Ireland's Children's Hospice **making the most of short and precious lives for more families**.

Or you can make a donation in any bank via IBAN to:

IBAN: IE38AIBK93357032130009
BIK: AIBKIE2D

Thanks for your support.

Sharon Morrow,
Chief Executive Officer,
LauraLynn, Ireland's Children's Hospice